STUDIEN ZUR ÖSTERREICHISCHEN PHILOSOPHIE

Herausgegeben von R. HALLER

Band III

RODERICK M. CHISHOLM

BRENTANO AND MEINONG STUDIES

Rodopi

1982

Printed in the Netherlands
ISBN: 90 6203 724 0

CONTENTS

FOREWORD

I present these papers on Brentano and Meinong in the hope that they will lead the reader back to the original sources. Some of the papers are expositions and commentaries. Others are developments of certain suggestions first made by Brentano or by Meinong.

The first two papers are concerned with the basic presuppositions of Brentano's theoretical philosophy. "Brentano's Theory of Substance and Accident" was presented to the Congress on the Philosophy of Franz Brentano held in Graz in September 1977; it first appeared in the *Grazer Philosophische Studien*, Vol. V (1978). The second paper — "Brentano's Theory of Judgment" — has not been published before; but a preliminary version of part of it, entitled "Brentano's Nonpropositional Theory of Judgment," appeared in the *Midwest Studies in Philosophy*, Vol. I (1976). It should be noted that Brentano's *Kategorienlehre*, to which many references are made in these two papers, has now been translated into English as *The Theory of Categories*, The Hague; Martinus Nijhoff 1981.

The third and fourth papers are concerned with Meinong's theory of objects, a theory that grows out of Brentano's theoretical philosophy. "Homeless Objects" first appeared in the Meinong issue of *Revue Internationale de Philosophie*, Vol. 22 (1973). "Beyond Being and Nonbeing" was presented to the Colloquium on Meinong that took place at the University of Graz in September and October, 1970. It first appeared in *Jenseits von Sein und Nichtsein*, edited by Rudolf Haller (Graz: Akademische Druck- und Verlagsanstalt, 1972). The paper makes clear, I think, that Russell's theory of descriptions — despite its great philosophical merit — does not provide a refutation of Meinong's theory.

The four papers that follow are concerned with the theory of value, as it had been conceived by Brentano and developed by Meinong. "Correct and Incorrect Emotion" and "The Quality of Pleasure and Displeasure" are both adapted from "Brentano's Theory of Correct and Incorrect Emotion," which first appeared in the Brentano issue of the *Revue Internationale de Philosophie*, Vol. 20 (1966). "Objectives and Intrinsic Value" is a revised version of a second paper that I presented to the Meinong Colloquium in 1970; the original version appears in *Jenseits von Sein und Nichtsein.*

"Supererogation and Offence" first appeared in *Ratio*, Vol. V (1963). In this work I make use, not only of certain insights of Meinong, but also those of one of his followers, Dr. Ernst Schwarz. Schwarz's excellent book, *Über den Wert, das Soll, und das richtige Werthalten*, has been almost entirely neglected. It was first brought to my attention by Hofrat Dr. Rudolf Kindinger who first introduced me to Graz.

The final paper — "Beginnings and Endings" — is a revision of a paper entitled "Brentano als analytischer Metaphysiker," which first appeared in the special volume of *Conceptus* entitled *Österreichische Philosophie und ihr Einfluss auf die analytische Philosophie der Gegenwart*, Jg. XI (1977), Nr. 28-30, pp. 77-82. A later version appeared in *Time and Cause*, edited by Peter Van Inwagen (Dordrecht: D. Reidel, 1980), pp. 17-25. It has been revised once again for the present volume.

I hope that these essays will be thought of as carrying out the tradition of the Brentano school.

It is especially gratifying for me to have them appear in Rudolf Haller's series, *Studien zur Österreichischen Philosophie*. If the papers have any philosophical merit, this is due in large part to the long and most rewarding association I have had with him and the University of Graz.

I wish to thank Leopold Stubenberg for his assistance in preparing the final manuscript.

BRENTANO'S THEORY OF SUBSTANCE AND ACCIDENT

1. *Introduction*

When Brentano, in the final reistic stage of his philosophy, lists what there is, the things that there are, in the strict sense of the expression "there are," he cites substances, aggregates of substances, and parts of substances. And along with these he cites something that he calls "accidents." Thus he writes, for example:

> Among beings in the strict sense of the term, there are to be included, not only every substance, every multiplicity of substances, and every part of a substance, but also every accident.[1]

Let us concentrate upon this concept of an accident. The word "accident," in this use, is not a part of the current philosophical vocabulary. And when we consider its traditional use, we may well wonder how such a concept fits into Brentano's reistic ontology. What kind of concretum, or *ens reale*, is an accident?

The examples that Aristotle had given are not very convincing. And at first consideration Brentano's are even less so. Thus when Brentano wants to illustrate what he means by "accident", he often appeals to the example of an atom having psychical attributes — an atom that can think and see and hear. There may not *be* such atoms, he says, but if there were, then they would illustrate the concept of an accident.

If the atom were to think, then there would be a thinker (*ein Denkendes*). This thinker would be an *accident* of the atom; it would be a thing that comes into being when the atom begins to think and that passes away when the atom ceases to think. And if the atom were to see and to hear, then there would be a seeing thing (*ein Sehendes*) and a hearing thing (*ein Hörendes*); the seeing thing and the hearing

1. "Ein Seiendes im eigentlichen Sinne ist nicht bloß jede Substanz, jede Mehrheit von Substanzen, und jeder Teil einer Substanz, sondern auch jedes Akzidens." *Kategorienlehre* (Hamburg: Felix Meiner, 1968), p. 11.

thing would be independent of each other in that either could exist without the other, but they would not be independent of the atom. The seeing thing and the hearing thing would be accidents of the atom.[2]

Now let us consider an actual case. Brentano says that when a *person* sees, or hears, or wills, then the self (*das Ich*) has as accidents a hearer, a see-er and a willer, and that these things may exist independently of each other, but not independently of the self. They are accidents and the self is the substance of those accidents.

To one who is accustomed to thinking in the categories presupposed by Peirce and Frege and Russell, all of this is somewhat bewildering. But I believe that, if we make a certain effort to view the world in the way Brentano does, we will see that he may well have something very important to teach us about substances and accidents and about ontology. And perhaps he has succeeded in making certain fundamental points that Aristotle was trying to make, but without the dubious concept of prime matter.

2. *The Primacy of the Intentional*

To understand Brentano's ontology, one must realize that he appeals to inner perception for his paradigmatic uses of the word "is." Inner perception has for its object our own intentional activity. It is immediately evident and is the source of our knowledge of the nature of being, just as it is the source of our knowledge of the nature of truth and of the nature of good and evil. What can be said about the being of things that are *not* apprehended in inner perception can be understood only by analogy with what we are able to say about ourselves as thinking subjects.

In constructing his ontology Brentano also appeals to those things — patches of color, sounds, smells and the like — that constitute the objects of our sensation. Brentano calls sensation "outer perception" and he calls the objects of sensation "physical phenomena," but in using this terminology he does not mean to imply that the objects of sensations are physical bodies that exist outside our own bodies; indeed he holds that they do not exist at all. To say that one "sees" a patch of color, according to Brentano, is not to say that there *is* a

2. See *Kategorienlehre*, p. 152; *Versuch über die Erkenntnis*, Second edition (Hamburg: Felix Meiner, 1970), p. 29.

patch of color that one sees. Sensation — or "outer perception" — is paradigmatically intentional: it has an object but that object does not exist.

Let us speak, then, of *the ontological primacy of the intentional* — meaning by this phrase that intentional phenomena, both "inner" perception and so-called "outer" perception, are what provide us with our data for ontology.

3. *Concrete Terms in Place of Predicates*

We will also speak of *the theory of concrete predication.* We will best understand this theory if, first, we imagine that all predicates in our language have been replaced by concrete terms, and if, secondly, we consider a view of the world which might naturally suggest itself to us if our language were in fact of such a sort — as it very well could have been.

There is no difficulty in principle in there being such a language. Thus English could be transformed into such a language somewhat artifically, by turning adjectives and verbs into concrete terms. In place of "red," for example, we could have "red-thing", and in place of "thinks," we could have "thing-that-is-thinking." (In the latter case, "thinker" is also available to us, but in its ordinary use it does not convey the activity suggested by "thing-that-is-thinking.") This move is less artifical in German than it is in English. And we find, especially in the writings of Brentano and the commentaries of Kraus and Kastil, a rich vocabulary of nouns that have been constructed from verbs and adjectives.

Given such a predicate-less vocabulary, we would say, not "Roses are red" and "All men are rational," but "Roses are red-things" and "All men are rational-beings" (or "All men are things-that-are rational").

Since we do say "Roses are red," it may be natural for us to suppose that, when someone believes or judges that roses are red, he is thereby predicating or attributing the property redness to roses. But if we say "Roses are red-things," then it may be more natural for us to suppose that, when someone believes or judges that roses are red-things, he is concerned not with a relation between things and properties, but with certain relations between things — between roses and red-things.

We may recall that this is what Aristotle had said of simple judgments: "An *affirmation* is a statement affirming something of something, a *negation* is a statement denying something of something."[3] In simple affirmative judgments, he said, we *combine* things and in simple negative judgments we *separate* them.[4]

Relational statements may be construed in a similar way. Instead of saying "Socrates is taller than Caius," we may say "Socrates is a thing-taller-than-Caius." The judgment which such a statement expressed may be thought of as combining Socrates with a certain *relativum.*

4. *Accidents as Individual Things*

To understand the use of the term "accident" to refer to what seems to be a type of individual thing, let us recall the traditional distinction between those determinations which are substantial and those which are accidental. The *substantial* determinations of an individual thing are those of its determinations which it cannot lose without ceasing to be; and the *accidental* determinations are those which are such that the individual can lose them and yet continue to be. "Accidental" is thus to be contrasted with "necessary": the accidental determinations of an individual thing are those which are not necessary for the thing's existence.

And now let us consider this distinction in the context of the theory of concrete predication we have just presupposed. The two types of determination — substantial and accidental — illustrate two different types of combination, two different ways in which "things may be affirmed of things."

Suppose, for example, we judge that a certain man is playing music — or, as we may now put it, that a certain man is a music-player. Here we have an accidental determination; the man need not thus be a music-player in order to exist (i.e., he need not be playing music in

3. *De Interpretatione* 16 a 11.

4. It should be noted that Brentano rejects this account of simple judgments. He rejects it because the simplest "thetic" affirmations ("He accepts horses," i.e., he judges that there are horses) are not concerned with *combining* things and because the simplest "thetic" denials ("He rejects unicorns," i.e., he judges that there are no unicorns) are not concerned with *separating* things. See *The True and the Evident* (London: Routledge and Kegan Paul, 1966), 16ff; *Wahrheit und Evidenz* (Hamburg: Felix Meiner, 1962), 18ff.

order to exist). Our judgment may be thought of as combining two things — a man and a music-player.

Suppose, then, that the man ceases to play music. Then he breaks off his relationship with the music-player. The man himself survives this change. But what happens to the music-player? Aristotle suggests that he ceases to be: "The musical man passed away and the unmusical man came to be, but the man persists as identically the same."[5]

Now we may assume that what ceases to be cannot subsequently come into being. As Locke said, there cannot be "two beginnings of existence." If, then, the musical man ceased to be when the man ceased to play music, then *that* musical man will not return to existence when the man begins to play again. Rather, the man will take on another accident: a new musical man will come into being.

A corollary of the foregoing will be the doctrine that Aristotelians have expressed by saying: an accident cannot be transferred from one subject to another. If you begin playing at the moment that I cease to play, then at one and the same moment one music-player will come into being and another will cease to be. But there is no possibility whatever of your taking on that music-player which had been an accident of me.

I bear an intimate relationship to my accidents, then. I have them and nothing else could possibly have them. They are all *my* accidents and they couldn't be those of anything else. But the intimate relationship is not that of identity. Each of my accidents is such that it is possible for me to exist without it.

5. *Substances as Parts of Accidents*

What ontologically intimate relationship is there other than identity? One such relationship, as Brentano saw, is that of whole to part. A proper part of a given whole is not identical with that whole, but the part is intimately related to the whole in the following sense: the whole — that particular whole — couldn't exist unless the part also existed. Can we understand the substance-accident relation in terms of part and whole?

To be sure, one wouldn't ordinarily say that the music player and the man are related as whole to part — or as part to whole. But

5. *Coming into Being and Passing Away*, 319b.

Brentano, we could say, takes the term "part" somewhat more widely than it is ordinarily taken. The relation that he calls that of part to whole is *analogous* to the relation that is ordinarily called that of part to whole; indeed, the ordinary relation may be exhibited as a subspecies of the relation that Brentano discusses.

In setting forth Brentano's theory, I will use the expressions "part" and "whole" in the broad sense that conforms to Brentano's intention. Then I will note how the ordinary sense of these expressions may be characterized by reference to this broad sense. And then, to avoid confusion between Brentano's use and the ordinary use, I will propose that the technical term "constituent" replace the term "part" in the statement of Brentano's theory.

Brentano says, then, that the relation of an accident to its subject is that of whole to part: the subject is a proper part of the accident. At first consideration, this may seem entirely out of line with the traditional conception. For, traditionally, the accident was thought of as dwelling *in* the subject; in the case of substance one could speak of *esse*, but in the case of accident one could speak only of *inesse.* And one may say that a proper part exists *within* its whole but not that the whole exists within the part. Yet Brentano has it just the other way around. According to him, the substance is a proper part of the accident and therefore, if proper parts exist within their wholes, one should say that the substance is "in" the accident and not that the accident is "in" the substance.

But the use of "in" in the statement of the traditional doctrine was metaphorical. It was used to express, not containment, but ontological dependence. The accident is in the substance in the sense that it is ontologically dependent upon the substance: the accident could not exist except as being accident of that particular substance. But wholes and parts are so related that the whole is ontologically dependent upon the part: the whole could not exist except as having that particular part. The principle of mereological essentialism — the principle that parts are essential to their wholes — is basic to Brentano's theory of substance and accident.

Now let us note a very special feature of that part-whole relation which is the substance-accident relation — a feature which, so far as I know, has been discussed only by Brentano.

6. *"One-sided Detachability"*

The substance-accident relation is not *merely* that of part to whole. It is a part-whole relation of a very special sort: it illustrates what Brentano calls "one-sided detachability (*einseitige Ablösbarkeit*)." This concept may be defined within the theory of part and whole.

Brentano observes that ordinary physical wholes — chairs, tables, organic bodies — are such that "any part can fall away while the other remains unchanged in every respect, except for its isolation."[6] And this means that such wholes lack the feature of one-sided detachability. This point may be put more exactly.

To have a positive understanding of one-sided detachability, let us first consider an analogue that Brentano provides for us and then turn to certain deliverances of inner perception.

The analogue is this:

> We can distinguish the concept colored in the concept red. But we cannot conceive what it would be to detach from the concept colored that which distinguishes red from any other color. And so we have here a case of a part which can be detached from a whole. Yet we cannot specify another part which, when combined with the first one, makes up that whole.[7]

The concept red, in other words, would seem to have the concept colored as a proper part. And yet it has no other part which is such that that other part in combination with the concept colored yields the concept red. Here, then, we have an analogue of one-sided detachability. Roughly speaking, we have a whole of this sort: it has a proper part — a part which is less than the whole — which is such that, if you detach only that part from the whole, then there will be nothing left.[8]

"One-sided detachability" is exhibited, perhaps somewhat more plausibly, by certain facts of inner perception.[9] These are the facts to which Brentano refers when he tells us that there are "accidents of accidents."

6. *Kategorienlehre*, p. 115.

7. *Kategorienlehre*, 151-2.

8. Why do we say that the example is only an analogue of one-sided detachability? According to Brentano, such ostensible entities as the concept red and the concept colored are fictions; what we say about such entities can be put in a less abbreviated way in terms of thinkers — thinkers of red-things and thinkers of colored-things.

9. Thus Kraus observes, in connection with von Ehrenfels' theory of "Gestalt Qualities," that the concept of a whole which is "not the sum of its parts" is one that has long been familiar. See his "Einige kritische Darlegungen," *Lotos Prag*, Band 69 (1921), 233-242; esp. 234.

7. *Accidents of Accidents*

Brentano puts the following question: Can things that are accidents be themselves subjects of still further accidents? And he answers it by reference to inner perception. And unlike Aristotle, he answers this question affirmatively. He tells us that "the relation of *being subject of* [*Subjektsverhältnis*] may hold not only between subject and accident, but also between accidents."[10]

In what follows, let us restrict ourselves to "absolute accidents" — to those accidents which are not *relativa*. Most of the familiar properties of physical things involve *relativa* — for such properties are relational. The clearest examples of absolute, non-relational accidents, are provided by inner perception. Let us consider knowing, judging, and thinking — or rather, those accidents of ourselves which are knowers, judgers, and thinkers.

Knowing or apprehending, according to Brentano's analysis, presupposes judging; but not conversely. And judging, in turn, presupposes thinking or having ideas; but not conversely. Let us put these points somewhat more precisely and in the type of notation we have been considering — a notation in which verbs and adjectives are replaced by nonabstract terms.

Thus we might say that every apprehender is a judger, but not conversely, and that every judger is one-who-is-thinking-of-something, but not conversely. The point may be made still more precisely by reference to the *intentional object* of the apprehender, the judger, and the one who is thinking of something. We could say, then: every *apprehender of horses* (everyone who knows that there are horses) is *an acceptor of horses* (one who believes that there are horses), and not conversely; and every *acceptor of horses* is one who is a *thinker of horses*, and not conversely. Let us also say, more simply: all apprehenders are judgers, and not conversely; and all judgers are thinkers, and not conversely.

What we are saying about apprehenders, judgers, and thinkers, is — up to a point — like what we might say of wolfhounds, dogs and animals. Every wolfhound is a dog, but not conversely; and every dog is an animal, but not conversely. Yet there is an important difference between the relation of apprehender to judger, on the one hand, and that of wolfhound to dog, on the other. And there is a similar

10. *Kategorienlehre*, p. 67, 150-1.

difference between the relation of dog to animal and the relation of judger to thinker.

There are animals which are not dogs. But if there is an animal which is not a dog, then it is an animal of some *other* species — some species of animal which is such that being a member of that species is incompatible with being a dog. And there are dogs which are not wolfhounds. But dogs which are not wolfhounds are dogs of another positive species — some species of dog which is incompatible with being a wolfhound.

An apprehender, however, may cease to be an apprehender and become just a judger; and a judger may cease to be a judger and become just a thinker. Thus Brentano writes:

> It is easy to see that what we are dealing with here is something essentially different from the unification of a generic and a specific determination. For the genus cannot be actual unless it is combined with a specific attribute which determines it. The genus can be separated from the species only in thought.[11]

"Accidents of accidents," then, provide us with clear cases of one-sided detachability.

8. *Brentano's Theory of Part and Whole*

To understand what Brentano is telling us, we must introduce the concept of a "proper part". We have been using "part" in such a way that every whole may be said to be a part of itself. A proper part of a whole would be a part that is not identical with the whole. In other words, if one thing is a proper part of another thing, then the first thing is part of the second thing but the second thing is not part of the first thing. Let us single out this concept by means of a definition, but one in which the technical term "constituent" replaces "part":

D1 x is a proper constituent of y = Df x is a constituent of y, and y is not a constituent of x.

We may say that the relation, *being a constituent of*, is like the relation, *being a part of*, in the following respects: (i) it is reflexive (everything bears it to itself); (ii) it is transitive (if one thing bears it to a second and the second to a third, then the first thing bears it to the third); and (iii) it is essentialistic in the following respect: if one thing bears it to another (is a part or constituent of the other), then the

11. *Kategorienlehre*, 149.

second thing is necessarily such that the first bears the relation to it (necessarily such that the first is a part or constituent of it).

Now when Brentano says that the relation of subject to accident manifests "one-sided detachability", he is telling us this: the accident is a whole which has the subject as one of its proper parts; but, although the subject is a *proper* part of the accident, the accident does not contain any *other* proper part — it does not contain any proper part in *addition* to the subject. That is to say, if the whole is the accident and the subject is the proper part, then every proper part of the accident is a part of the subject — or in other words, every proper part of the accident is either identical with the subject or is a part of the subject.

And so we may define the concept of an accident in the following way.

D2 x is an accident of y = Df y is a proper constituent of x, and every proper constituent of x is a constituent of y.

Brentano says, in accordance with the traditional conception, that an accident is a being "which requires another being as its subject."[12] We see now that it "requires" its subject in the sense that it is a whole which requires its subject as a part or constituent. Every whole, we have said, has its parts or constituents necessarily. And so we may say that the accident would not exist unless its subject were to exist.

The relation of accident to subject is thus not illustrated by the ordinary part-whole relations which obtain among physical things. If one physical thing is a proper part of another, then the second physical thing has still other proper parts, entirely discrete from the first one.

Yet, Brentano says, it is evident on the basis of inner perception that there are things which are accidents of other things.

Given the concept of an accident, we should now be in a position to say what a substance is, for "substance is to be contrasted with accident."[13]

Shall we say, then, that a substance is that which has an accident? This is what Aristotle had held, according to Brentano's interpretation: substance is "the bearer of accidents."[14] But this account of substance is unsatisfactory for two reasons: first, substances are *not*

12. *Kategorienlehre*, 219.
13. *Kategorienlehre,* 146.
14. "Trägerin der Akzidentien"; *Kategorienlehre*, 139.

the only things that have accidents (for accidents may have accidents); and, secondly, it is possible, according to Brentano, that there are substances that do not have any accidents.

Sometimes Brentano characterizes substances purely negatively. He says, for example: "The term substance is applicable to a thing only to the extent that the thing is not an accident."[15] But this should not be taken strictly, since, according to Brentano, *boundaries* are neither substances nor accidents. I suggest that it is in the spirit of Brentano's intention to say rather this: a substance is a thing that is not itself an accident but is capable of having accidents.

D3 x is a substance = Df x is possibly such that it has an accident, and x is not an accident.

We have said that it is evident on the basis of inner perception that there are accidents. But can we be sure that there are *substances*? Might not there be just accidents of accidents *ad infinitum*? This possibility is ruled out by a further *a priori* principle which is basic to Brentano's metaphysics — the principle, namely, that there cannot be an infinite number of things. Given this principle, we must say that, if there is an accident, then there is "an ultimate subsisting part (*ein letztes Subsistierendes*)". Hence, Brentano also suggests an alternative account of substance: "Now, the ultimate subsisting part, the part that subsists without containing any part that subsists, is called the substance."[16]

God would not be a substance by these definitions, for God is not capable of having accidents. But, as Brentano observes, this consequence is as it should be. The word "substance" was introduced in philosophy to refer to that which "substands" or "subsists" — to that which underlies accidents. If we restrict "substance" to this original sense, then we might say that God resembles substances in this respect; he is a "primary individual" (Brentano's expression is "*ein Wesen*").[17]

15. *Kategorienlehre*, p. 146. This leads Kastil to observe that "substance" is not a genuine name, since "there are no negative ideas." A genuine name, according to Kastil, would be: "a substance-container," i.e. "a thing which contains a substance (*ein etwas als Substanz Einschliessendes*)." See the editorial notes to the *Kategorienlehre*, pp. 345 (note 1a) and 399 (note 40).

16. *Kategorienlehre*, 150. But Brentano resists the temptation to define substance as that which has no proper parts. In connection with this, compare *Kategorienlehre*, 145-6; 143.

17. See *Kategorienlehre*, 43.

What, then, is a primary individual?

Should we say that a primary individual is a thing that is not an accident? This would have the consequence that spatial boundaries — lines, surfaces, and points — are primary individuals. But these things, Brentano says, are not entities in their own right; they exist only to the extent that they are parts of other things. (A point exists only if it is part of a line, a line only if it is a part of a surface, and a surface only if it is part of a body). "Just as it is certain that there are boundaries and that they must be included among things, it is also certain that a boundary is not a thing existing in itself [*nicht etwas für sich Bestehendes*]. The boundary could not exist unless it belonged as boundary to a continuum."[18] What is it, then, for a thing to be such that it exists in itself?

We have said, in effect, that wholes are things which need to *have* parts. We could also say that boundaries — those things which do not exist in themselves — are things that need to *be* parts. Hence a thing exists in itself if it is a thing which is capable of existing without being a proper part of another thing:

D4 x exists in itself (*ist etwas für sich*) = Df x is possibly such that there is nothing of which it is a proper constituent.

Brentano also uses the expression "a thing for itself (*ein Ding für sich*)."[19]

We may now say that a primary individual is a thing which is such that it doesn't need to *have* a part and it doesn't need to *be* a part. In other words, a primary individual is something that exists in itself and is not an accident:

D5 x is a primary individual (*ein Wesen*) = Df x exists in itself and is not an accident.

Brentano had held, at least for a while, that physical bodies are primary individuals which are not substances. Thus he writes in one place: "Whether bodies ... underlie real accidents and thus constitute their substances is open to doubt, particularly if bodies are incapable of mental activity. In any case, bodies are not themselves accidents; rather they are such that each of their parts is separable from the others, and this separability is reciprocal. In this respect they are like

18. *Kategorienlehre*, p. 170.
19. *Kategorienlehre*, p. 158.

substances, and we can say that like substances they are primary individuals."[20]

Given the concept of a primary individual, we are now in a position to define the *ordinary* sense of the word "part." The part-relation is a subspecies of the constituent relation; it is, namely, the constituent relation insofar as it holds among primary individuals:

D6 x is a part of y = Df x and y are primary individuals, and x is a constituent of y.

Hence if one thing is a proper *part* — as distinct from being a proper *constituent* — of another thing, then the second thing is an aggregate, and it is an aggregate that is not susceptible to one-sided detachability.[21]

What, then, is an aggregate (or *Kollektivum*)? I believe it would be in the spirit of what Brentano has said to define an aggregate as a primary individual which has a primary individual as a proper constituent:

D7 x is an aggregate (*Kollektivum*) = Df x is a primary individual which has a primary individual as a proper constituent.

Is an aggregate a substance? Brentano says in one place: "I would say that a body, a mind, and a god are substances. But I would also say that a multiplicity (*Mehrheit*) composed of bodies, or of minds, or of a mind together with a body fall under the concept of a substance."[22]

Brentano also uses the expression "ultimate substance (*letzteinheitliche Substanz*)"[23] Presumably an ultimate substance would be a

20. *Kategorienlehre*, p. 153. But in a dictation of 1915, included as an appendix to the *Kategorienlehre* (pp. 296-300), Brentano suggests "that the totality of what is corporeal might be conceived as a single bodily substance which is at rest (*als eine einzige ruhende Körpersubstanz*)" and that the physical bodies studied by the natural sciences are accidents of this single substance.

21. This definition of "part" has the consequence that spatial boundaries are not parts of bodies. And so our observation above — that boundaries need to *be* parts — should be modified by saying that they need to be *constituents*: they are necessarily such that they are constituents of bodies. They may also be constituents of other boundaries.

22. *Kategorienlehre*, 145-6.

23. See *Kategorienlehre*, pp. 249, 270. He sometimes also uses "ultimate subject (*letzteinheitliches Subject*)"; compare, p. 230.

substance having no substance as a proper constituent. Hence we might say:

D8 x is an ultimate substance (*eine letzte einheitliche Substanz*) = Df x is a substance which is not an aggregate.

According to Brentano's ontology, then, there are five types of *being*, or *thing*. These are: (1) *boundaries* — things which need to be constituents of other things; (2) *accidents* — things which need to have other things as their constituents; (3) *aggregates* — things which have as constituents things which do not need to be constituents; (4) *ultimate substances* — things which are neither accidents nor aggregates, but which could be proper constituents; and (5) *primary individuals which are not substances* — things which cannot be constituents and which do not need to have constituents. God would be a primary individual that is not a substance.

BRENTANO'S THEORY OF JUDGMENT

Introduction

In the final reistic phase of his thought Brentano rejects such *entia irrealia* as propositions, judgmental contents, and states of affairs, and he develops what may be called a "nonpropositional theory of judgment". It is normally supposed that a nonpropositional theory of judgment cannot possibly be made adequate to so-called compound judgments. I shall attempt to show that this supposition is false.

The two essential features of Brentano's theory of judgment are these: (1) that there are two irreducibly different types of judgment, one affirmative and the other negative; and (2) that the only terms needed in the formulation of such judgments are terms that a reist could countenance as being genuine.

Genuine Terms

What would be such a genuine term? If we are reists, we will say that the only genuine terms there are are terms that refer to *entia realia* — for example, to individuals and other concrete things. More exactly, our genuine terms will be such that, if they refer to anything, then that thing will be an *ens reale.* Thus even though there are no unicorns or mermaids, the terms "unicorn" and "mermaid" may be genuine terms: if they were to refer, then they would refer to *entia realia.*

Given this concept of a genuine term, let us extend it recursively in accordance with the following formula.

If *T* is a genuine term, then: (i) *T-acceptor, T-rejector, correct-T-acceptor* and *correct-T-rejector* are genuine terms; (ii) *part-of-T* is a genuine term; and (iii) if *R* is a genuine term, then the following are genuine terms: (a) *T-which-is-R*, (b) *T-and-R*, and (c) *T-or-R.*

Let us now consider each of the classes in this formula.

We may use the term "acceptor" to refer to a person who makes a positive judgment and the term "rejector" to refer to a person who makes a negative judgment. Since "horse" is a term, "horse-acceptor" will refer to a person who makes a positive judgment with respect to horses. Such a person would be described in our ordinary propositional locution by saying he "believes that there are horses," but in Brentano's terms he would be one who "accepts horses", or more simply a "horse-acceptor." The term "horse-rejector," analogously, would refer to one who makes a negative judgment with respect to horses. We would describe such a person in our ordinary propositional locution as one who believes that there are no horses.

We may also qualify these terms with the word "correct." The notion of *being correct* is essential to Brentano's theory of knowledge and truth as well as to his theory of ethics. Since there are horses, all horse-acceptors are correct horse-acceptors and there are no correct-horse-rejectors. Since there are no unicorns, all unicorn-rejectors are correct-unicorn-rejectors and there are no correct-unicorn-acceptors.

If "horse" is a genuine term, then "part-of-horse" (or as we may say more easily "part of a horse") is a genuine term. In his later writings, Brentano holds, in opposition to Aristotle, that parts of *entia realia* are themselves *entia realia*, and he holds in opposition to Leibniz that aggregates of *entia realia* are also *entia realia.*

Genuine terms may be combined to make new genuine terms. Thus we have said that, if *T* and *R* are genuine terms, then *T-which-is-R* is a genuine term. If "man" and "mortal" are genuine terms, then "man-which-is-mortal" is a genuine term. And there is no significant difference between "T-which-is-R" and "R-which-is-T."

Again, if *T* and *R* are genuine terms, then *T-and-R* is a genuine term. Since "horse" is a genuine term and "man" is a genuine term, then "horse-and-man" is a genuine term. This point is connected with what might be called Brentano's *conjunctivism* — his doctrine that, if A is an *ens reale* and B is an *ens reale*, then there is an *ens reale* having A and B as parts. If there is a horse and if there is a man, then there is a horse-and-man which is itself neither a horse nor a man. Thus an A-and-B may not be an A-which-is-B, but presumably any A-which-is-B is also an A-and-B. An A-and-B is a *conjunctivum*, or *collectivum*, which contains an A as well as a B; but, as in the case of that *collectivum* which is a horse and a dog, the one need not be predicable of the other. However, in the case of an A-which-is-a-B — say, a dog which is a brown thing — the one thing *is* predicable of the other.

We have said, finally, that if *T* and *R* are genuine terms, then *T-or-R* is a genuine term. This doctrine enables us to extend Brentano's nonpropositional theory of judgment in such a way that it will apply to certain compound judgments he does not consider, but it is not a doctrine that Brentano emphasizes. He does say: "A plurality of things may be so combined in one idea that each of the things is conceived of as 'one or the other of the several things.' Here we have a distinctive concept which is predicable of each of the things, however different they may be in other respects. Thus, having connected a man and a dog in thought, I form the idea of 'either one of the two.' In such cases, one speaks of *disjunctive* concepts."[1] We spoke of conjunctivism in connection with conjunctive terms above; here we could speak of the associated doctrine of *disjunctivism*. As the quotation from Brentano suggests, a man is a man-or-dog and a dog is a man-or-dog. We could also say (though Brentano says nothing like this) that every man is a man-or-unicorn and nothing other than a man is a man-or-unicorn.

We shall, for the present, defer the question whether *negative terms* — such as "non-man" — are needed in Brentano's account.

"Thetic" Judgments

Katkov observes that "almost simultaneously with his rupture with the Church, Brentano discovered that he could not follow Aristotle in one of the most basic tenets of his philosophy. He thought Aristotle had overlooked or misinterpreted an essential element of the function of the mind which finds its expression in enunciated propositions to which the terms 'true' and 'false' are applied in the proper sense of the words. In other words, he thought Aristotle's definition of judgment, as the combination of ideas which is true if things corresponding to the ideas are connected, and false if they are

1. Franz Brentano, *Kategorienlehre* (Hamburg: Felix Meiner, 1968), ed. Alfred Kastil, p. 45. But Kastil, commenting on this passage, says: "These so-called disjunctive concepts are neither real pedicates nor genuine concepts; they are synsemantic"; p. 313, note 7. And Brentano himself seems to reject disjunctivism in other passages. See, for example, *Psychologie vom empirischen Standpunkt*, Band II (Hamburg: Felix Meiner Verlag), p. 247; *Psychology from an Empirical Standpoint* (London: Routledge & Kegan Paul, 1973), p. 346. We shall note below that, in his lectures on logic, Brentano had proposed a somewhat different treatment of disjunctions.

disconnected, omitted the most essential feature of what a judgment is, namely the element of belief, that is of assertion or negation. An assertion or negation can be true or false without encompassing a combination of two ideas, as when we say that something is or that it is not."[2]

The simplest judgments are those involving concepts that are not compound. These are what Marty was to call "thetic" judgments and are either affirmative or negative.[3]

What may be called a *thetic affirmation* is a judgment which, as we may be tempted to say, "affirms the existence" of certain *entia realia.* An example is the judgment which we would express propositionally by saying "He believes that there are horses." But this thetic affirmation, according to Brentano's theory, may be put in non-propositional form by saying "He accepts horses." And we may say, more generally:

(D1) He judges that there are A's =Df He accepts A's.

(In this definition and in those that follow, the left-hand sentence, containing the subordinate propositional clause, is defined in Brentano-type terminology by means of sentences containing no subordinate propositional clauses.)

The most elementary affirmative thetic judgments are manifested in sensation. It is impossible, according to Brentano, to experience the content of sensation without, *ipso facto* affirming its existence.

The second type of simple thetic judgment might be called a *thetic denial*. An example is the judgment expressed by "He believes that there are no unicorns," a judgment which, as we may be tempted to say, "affirms the nonexistence" of unicorns. But according to Brentano, such a judgment doesn't affirm anything; it simply denies or rejects unicorns. Using "rejects" to express such negative judgments, we may add this definition:

(D2) He judges that there are no A's =Df He rejects A's.

Brentano thus assumes that there are two fundamental types of judgment, acceptance and rejection, neither of which can be reduced

2. George Katkov, "The World in which Franz Brentano Believed he Lived," *Grazer Philosophische Studien*, Vol. V (1978), pp. 13-27; see p. 13.

3. See Anton Marty, "Über subjektlose Sätze und das Verhältnis der Grammatik zur Logik und Psychologie: Siebenter Artikel," *Vierteljahrschrift für wissenschaftliche Philosophie*, Band 19 (1895), 263-334; see page 298.

to the other. Acceptance and rejection are contraries in the sense in which red and green are contraries. Or, more exactly, "S accepts A" and "S rejects A" will be contraries if the same term replaces "A" in each. Thus Brentano could accept the following observation by Aristotle:

> For it is impossible for any one to believe the same thing to be and not to be, as some think Heraclitus says. For what a man says, he does not necessarily believe; and if it is impossible that contrary attributes should belong at the same time to the same subject (the usual qualifications must be presupposed in this premise too), and if an opinion which contradicts another is contrary to it, obviously it is impossible for the same man at the same time to believe the same thing to be and not to be...[4]

How are we to interpret Aristotle's remark that "an opinion which contradicts another is contrary to it"? Given a propositional interpretation of the objects of belief, we could say that one opinion "contradicts" another provided that the propositional *objects* of the two opinions contradict each other: then we could say that the two doxastic *acts* are contrary if their *objects* are thus contradictory. (The two *acts* will be contrary and not contradictory, since it is possible for neither to occur.) On Brentano's view, we could say that two judgments contradict each other if the one accepts what the other rejects. Two acts of judgment which contradict each other will themselves be contraries, for they cannot both be made (that is to say, one and the same person cannot make both judgments at one and the same time): but the two acts of judgment will not be contradictory, for it is possible that neither is made.

Double Judgments

According to Brentano's earlier conception, judgments may be divided into those which accept a certain content and those which simply reject or deny a certain content. But according to his later conception, acceptance may be accompanied by one or the other of two additional attitudes — one of them affirming something further of the content accepted and the other denying something of the content accepted. The two expressions, "accept [*Anerkennen*]" and "reject [*Verwerfen*]" are to be supplemented by the two further expressions, "*Zuerkennen*" and "*Absprechen*" The expression "*Zu-*

4. *Metaphysics*, 1005b, 23ff.

erkennen" may be rendered somewhat roughly as "to predicate something of something," and "*Absprechen*" as "to deny something of something."

These locutions express what Brentano called "double judgments [*Doppelurteilen*]." These are "judgments in which something is first accepted as existing and in which something else is then either affirmed or denied *of* the first thing."[5] I make a double judgment when (i) I make a simple ("thetic") affirmative judgment which I can express in the form "There is an S" and (ii) I then supplement this affirmation either by a further *Zuerkennen* ("and what's more it is a P") or by an *Absprechen* ("and what's more it is not a P"). If an I-judgment ("Some S is P") is interpreted as a double judgment, then the judger has (i) accepted an S and (ii) has predicated P of S. And if an O-judgment ("Some S is not P") is interpreted as a double judgment, then the judger has (i) accepted an S and (ii) has denied P of S. The O-judgment, according to this conception, *is* an affirmative judgment, since it is a matter of accepting an S. Yet Brentano concedes, it is partly negative in that "it is a kind of denial in which something is denied of a thing which is affirmed [*eine Art Absprechen ... bei welchem das, dem etwas abgesprochen wird, anerkannt wird*]"[6] The I judgment, on this interpretation, does coincide with what Aristotle had called combinings or judgments of synthesis. And the O-judgments would seem to coincide with what he called the *diairesis* of subject and predicate.

Kraus has suggested that such double-judgments, because they involve a conceptual synthesis, might properly be "synthetic judgments."[7] But "synthetic" here contrasts with "thetic," rather than with "analytic." Kraus also observes that such double judgments provide us with one way of distinguishing between the subject and the predicate of a judgment: the *subject* of a double-judgment is that *of*

5. *The Origin of Our Knowledge of Right and Wrong* (London: Routledge & Kegan Paul, 1939), p. 107; *Psychologie vom empirischen Standpunkt*, Band II, 193-4. The passage is from the essay, "Miklosich über Subjektlose Sätze," which appears in the German edition of the *Psychologie* and is translated in the English edition of *The Origin of our Knowledge of Right and Wrong*.

6. *Vom Sinnlichen und Noetischen Bewusstsein* (Hamburg: Felix Meiner Verlag, 1968), p. 9.

7. See *Psychologie vom empirischen Standpunkt*, Vol. II, p. 300. The note here referred to does not appear in the English edition.

which something is affirmed or denied, and the *predicate* of such a judgment is that which is thus affirmed or denied of the subject.[8]

The Four Traditional Forms of Judgment

Brentano is now able to extend his analysis to the traditional A, E, I, and O judgments.

The simplest of these is the *I-judgment.* Like simple thetic affirmation, it is an acceptance, but unlike simple thetic affirmation it involves a compound of two terms. We may treat the I-judgment as a complex thetic judgment:

(D3) He judges that some S are P =Df He accepts an S which is a P.

Or we may treat the I-judgment as a double-judgment:

(D3′) He judges that some S are P =Df He accepts an S and predicates a P of it.

In the notation suggested above, the definiens of D3 would be "He accepts S-which-is-P." The expressions "S-which-is-P" and "P-which-is-S" are interchangable; hence Brentano says there is no significant distinction between the subjects and predicates of such judgments. It is important to note that the above definition, like those that follow, is a definition of a certain type of *judgment* and not a definition of a certain type of *proposition*. Thus (D3) above is a definition of judgments of the form "He judges that some S are P," and not a definition of propositions of the form "Some S are P."

We have already noted that the *O-judgment* is a double-judgment involving an *Absprechen*:

(D4) He judges that some S is not P =Df He is an acceptor of one who correctly denies P of an S.

If negative terms are admitted, then the O-judgment may be con-

8. Op. cit., p. 300. Evidently Brentano had two different psychological interpretations of the "synthesis" that takes place in the case of an I judgment. According to the one, the synthesis does express a two-fold judgment — first, a simple *Anerkennen* and then a *Zuerkennen* or an *Absprechen*. According to the other interpretation, the synthesis takes place wholly within the sphere of ideas and the judgment is simply an affirmation of the result. See Kastil's notes to the *Kategorienlehre* (Hamburg: Felix Meiner Verlag, 1968), p. 371. See also Marty's *Untersuchungen zur Grundlegung der allgemeinen Grammatik und Sprachphilosophie*, p. 341ff., and his *Gesammelte Schriften*, Vol. II, Part I, p. 227ff. and 309ff.

strued, not as a double-judgment, but as a thetic acceptance:

(D4′) He judges that some S is not P =Df He accepts an S which is a non-P.

The *E-judgment*, like the thetic denial, is a rejection; but unlike the thetic denial it involves a compound of two terms:

(D5) He judges that no S are P =Df He rejects S's which are P's.

The definiens may also be read as "He rejects S-which-is-P".

It would seem to be impossible to interpret the *A-judgment* without the use of negative terms. If such terms are admitted, then we may say that the *A-judgment* is like the E-judgment in that it is a rejection involving a compound of two terms. It differs from the E-judgment in that one of the two terms in the compound is negative.

(D6) He judges that all S are P =Df He rejects S's which are non-P's.

We could also say "He rejects S-which-is-non-P." This definition presupposes that it is not possible to dispense with negative terms in Brentano's nonpropositional theory of judgment.

According to the traditional account, the A-judgment and the I-judgment are affirmative, the E-judgment and the O-judgment are negative, the A-judgment and the E-judgment are universal, and the I-judgment and the O-judgment are particular. But Brentano says that one judges affirmatively if one accepts something and one judges negatively if one rejects something. Hence, given this terminology, he can say that the universal judgments, A and E, are negative and the particular judgments, I and O, are affirmative.

In an early discussion of Brentano's *Psychologie*, J.P.N. Land had noted that normally, when we use a *sentence* of the "All S is P" form, our use *presupposes* the existence of S's.[9] Brentano conceded this point, saying that "the ambiguity of our language allows us to use a simple categorical statement to express a plurality of judgments."[10] An "All S is P" sentence, then, may be used to express two judgments: (i) the thetic affirmation of an S and (ii) the rejection of S's which are non-P's.

Frege had rejected the view that there is a fundamental distinction

9. J.P.N. Land, "On a Supposed Improvement in Formal Logic," *Abhandlungen der königlichen Niederländischen Akademie der Wissenschaften*, 1876.

10. *The True and the Evident* (London: Routledge & Kegan Paul, 1966), p. 36; *Wahrheit und Evidenz* (Hamburg: Felix Meiner Verlag, 1962), p. 92.

between affirmative and negative judgments. He wrote: "What is more, it is by no means easy to state what is a negative judgment (thought). Consider the sentences 'Christ is immortal,' 'Christ lives for ever,' 'Christ is not immortal,' 'Christ is mortal,' 'Christ does not live for ever.' Now which of the thoughts we have here is affirmative, which negative?"[11] But if we take these sentences in their ordinary way, there is no problem, given Brentano's theory, in deciding which ones are affirmative and which are negative: they are *all* affirmative.

We have noted that, given Brentano's theory of judgment, two judgments may be said to contradict each other if they have the *same* object but one accepts it and the other rejects it. According to the propositional conception, A and O *propositions* contradict each other, and E and I propositions contradict each other. Looking at our definitions, we can see that, given Brentano's conception, the A-judgment rejects what the O-judgment accepts (namely, S's which are non-P's), and the E-judgment rejects what the I-judgment accepts (namely, S's which are P's).

Given that the *act* of accepting a certain object is the contrary of the *act* of rejecting that object, Brentano is able to say — what we cannot say on the propositional theory of judgment — that it is *impossible* for a man to make contradictory judgments at one and the same time; that is to say, it is impossible at one and the same time both to accept a certain object and also to reject that object.

Compound Judgments

We now turn to compound judgments. A compound judgment presupposes a compound thought. "If the thinking is a compound thought, then things are what one has compounded."[12] Brentano's own theory is not fully developed. I will suggest an account that is in the spirit of what Brentano says.

It will be instructive to consider Brentano's theory by reference to the six types of "compound thought" distinguished by Frege.[13] These are suggested by the following formulae:

11. G. Frege, "Negation," in P. Geach und Max Black, eds., *Translations from the Philosophical Writings of Gottlob Frege* (Oxford: Basil Blackwell, 1952); the quotation is on p. 125; *Kleine Schriften* (Hildesheim: Georg Olms, 1967), p. 369.

12. *The True and the Evident*, p. 83; *Wahrheit und Evidenz*, p. 93.

13. Gottlob Frege, "Compound Thoughts," *Mind*, lxii (1963), 1-17; "Gedankengefüge," *Kleine Schriften*, 378-394.

(1) A and B;
(2) Not-(A and B);
(3) Not-A and not-B;
(4) Not-(not-A and not-B); i.e., A or B;
(5) Not-A and B;
(6) Not-(not-A and B); i.e., A or B; if B then A

The simplest type of conjunctive judgment would be a *conjunctive affirmation*, and this is instanced by Frege's first type of "compound thought". Thus a person may judge that there are horses as well as cows. His conjunctive judgment is not merely a conjunction of judgments. In saying that the man judges in this way we are not saying merely that the man judges there are horses and also judges there are cows. We are saying that he has put two and two together, so to speak, and believes that there are both horses and cows. To fit this conjunctive judgment into Brentano's scheme, we appeal to his doctrine of conjunctivism. This doctrine enables us to say that, if there are horses and if there are cows, then there are those *conjunctiva* which are composed of horses and cows. Since "horse" is a genuine term and "cow" is a genuine term, we may also say, in accordance with what was set forth above, that "horse and cow" is a genuine term. And so we might analyse conjunctive affirmation this way:

(D7) He judges that there are A's and there are B's =Df He accepts (A and B)'s.

We may also say "He accepts A-and-B."

There are also *conjunctive denials*, as in "He believes that there are no mermaids and there are no unicorns." Here, too, the man may put two and two together; instead of merely rejecting unicorns and rejecting mermaids, he notes, so to speak, that both are wanting. To accomodate this type of judgment to our nonpropositional scheme, we may appeal to the doctrine of disjunctivism set forth above — the doctrine according to which, if there are A's, then there are those things which are (A-or-B)'s. A conjunctive denial, then, will be the rejection of such *disjunctiva.* In other words:

(D8) He judges that there are neither A's nor B's =Df He rejects (A-or-B)'s.

We may also say: "He rejects A-or-B". Here we have an instance of Frege's *third* type of "compound thought."

A *disjunctive affirmation* will thus be the affirmation of such a disjunctivum. Thus

(D9) He judges that there are A's or there are B's =Df He accepts (A-or-B)'s.

Thus to say that a man believes there are either unicorns or mermaids is consistent with saying that he believes there are unicorns but not mermaids; it is consistent with saying that he believes there are mermaids and not unicorns; and it is consistent with saying that he believes there are both unicorns and mermaids. Thus we have Frege's fourth type of "compound thought".

Brentano had also suggested a somewhat different interpretation of disjunctive judgments. According to this interpretation, when we judge that either there are A's or there are B's, we consider the collectivum, *an-A-and-a-B*, and judge that a part of it exists.[14] Given that, if A is a term, then "a part-of-an-A" is a term, we could express the definition this way:

> He judges that there are A's or there are B's =Df He accepts a part of an-A-and-a-B.

One may ask, however: is it possible to accept a part of an A-and-a-B without thereby accepting either an A or a B? What if one accepts merely a part of an A, or a part of a B? It would seem that disjunctive terms, like negative terms, are essential to Brentano's account.

There can also be *disjunctive denial*, as is evidenced by the man who believes that either there are no horses or there are no cows. Although I have called this type of judgment "disjunctive denial" (I say "disjunctive" because of the presence of the "or"), actually it may be said to involve the rejection of a conjunctivum — in our example that conjunctivum which is horse-and-cow. Hence:

(D10) He judges that either there are no A's or there are no B's =Df He rejects (A-and-B)'s.

This is an instance of Frege's second type of "compound thought".

Some compound judgments would seem to be composed of both positive and negative elements. Frege suggests that such judgments present special difficulties for the theory according to which judgments may be classified as being either affirmative or negative. Consider the man who believes that either there are *no* horses or there *are* cows. He is rejecting horses not outright but only on the condition that there be cows. And he is accepting cows not outright but only on the condition that there be no horses. As Brentano puts it, the man would be saying there are no horses "without cows."[15] I

14. Compare *Die Lehre vom richtigen Urteil* (Hamburg: Felix Meiner Verlag, 1956), p. 122.

15. See the *Psychology*, p. 300; *Psychologie*, Band II, 171.

suggest we may call this judgment a *conditional affirmation* and put it in nonpropositional terms as follows:

(D11) He judges that either there are no A's or there are B's =Df He rejects A's which are not parts of (A and B)'s.

If there are no horses without cows, then there are no horses which are not parts of horse-and-cow's. The definens is an application of our rule according to which if *T* is a genuine term, then *part-of-T* is a genuine term and *non-T* is a genuine term. Thus we have an instance of Frege's sixth type of "compound thought".

Let us now consider those compound judgments which could be said to be *combined affirmations and denials.* Consider a man who believes that there are horses and no cows. It is not merely that he believes that there are horses and that he believes there are no cows; he, too, puts two and two together and holds that, whereas there is the one, there isn't the other. How can such a combined affirmation and denial be viewed simply as an acceptance or as a rejection? It could be viewed as an acceptance of this sort:

(D12) He judges that there are A's and there are no B's =Df He accepts A's which are not parts of (A-and-B)'s.

An alternative definition, which fits well with a number of other things that Brentano says, would be this:

(D12′) He judges that there are A's and there are no B's =Df He accepts (A and correct-B-rejectors)'s.

One might defend this by saying that if the man judges that there are no B's (and is thus a B-rejector), he also judges that there are correct-B-rejectors (he himself would be one, or so he thinks. Brentano observes that "everyone who accepts or rejects something believes of himself that he accepts or rejects correctly; if he did not believe this of himself, he would not be judging at all."[16]

Let us add the following to our list:

(D13) He judges that there are S's and none of them are P's =Df He accepts an S-acceptor who is a correct S-and-P rejector.

The S-acceptor whom he thus accepts will be the judger himself. And that this judger is a *correct* S-and-P rejector will be a part of the content of his judgment.

We see, then, that Brentano's theory may accomodate each of Frege's six types of compound thought.

16. *The True and the Evident*; *Wahrheit und Evidenz*, p. 94, p. 85.

These various types of compound judgments may be combined in various ways. Let us consider just one example — a combination of conjunctive affirmation and conditional affirmation:

(D14) He judges that there are A's and there are B's and either there are no C's or there are D's =Df He accepts (A and (B and (correct rejectors of C's which are not parts of C and D's)))

More complex types of judgment may also be expressed within this nonpropositional theory. As Brentano suggests, however, it may be questioned whether people actually do make judgments of greater complexity than those illustrated here. A man may say, for example, that he accepts propositions of the form of *5.23 of *Principia Mathematica*; i.e.,

$$[\neg(p\epsilon q) \vee (\neg p\epsilon\neg q)] <=> [(p\epsilon\neg q) \vee (q\epsilon\neg p)]$$

But in all probability his judgment is about the formula itself. Thus if Brentano is right, the man is judging that there is a correct *5.23 acceptor, namely the man himself.[17]

If both negative and disjunctive terms are admitted, then all judgments may be reduced to thetic judgments. Thus Brentano wrote:

> I think I have shown in my *Psychology* that *every* judgment, whether it be expressed in categorical, hypothetical, or disjunctive form, may be expressed without loss of meaning in the form of a subjectless proposition, or, as I would prefer to put it, in the form of an existential proposition.[18]

It is clear that Brentano uses "existential proposition" both for the affirmative form "There are A's" and for the negative form "There are no A's."

Apodictic Judgments

In the "table of judgments" that Kant sets forth in the *Critique of*

17. In such a case, according to Brentano, the concept of the formula is a *surrogate* for that which the formula is intended to express. Again, a judgment ostensibly about the number 31,157,435 is likely to be a judgment about that numerical expression, for no one has a proper idea of that which is expressed by "31,157,435." Compare *Kategorienlehre*, p. 48; *The True and the Evident*, 83; *Wahrheit und Evidenz*, 92; and Alfred Kastil, *Die Philosophie Franz Brentanos* (Bern: A. Francke, 1951), pp. 60-61.

18. *The Origin of our Knowledge of Right and Wrong*, p. 106; *Psychologie*, Band II, 193.

Pure Reason, he distinguishes judgments with respect to four different features — *quantity* (universal, particular, and singular); *quality* (affirmative, negative, and infinite); *relation* (categorical, hypothetical, disjunctive); and *modality* (problematic, assertoric, and apodictic). The distinguishing characteristic of the *modality* of judgments, he says, is "that it contributes nothing to the content of the judgment..., but concerns only the value of the copula in relation to thought in general. Problematic judgments are those in which affirmation or negation is taken as merely possible (optional). In assertoric judgments affirmation or negation is viewed as real (true), and in apodictic judgments as necessary."[19]

Kant formulates his table of categories by reference to his table of judgments. Corresponding to the *problematic* judgment, there are the two categories, *possibility* and *impossibility*; corresponding to the *assertoric* judgment, there are the two categories, *existence* and *non-existence*; and corresponding to the *apodictic judgment*, there are the two categories, *necessity* and *contingency.*[20]

But if we view judgments as Brentano does, the correlation of type of judgment with modal category would be somewhat different.

Brentano sometimes says that apodictic judgments are those judgments "which either accept something as *necessary* or reject something as *impossible.*"[21] But he does not *define* apodictic judgments by reference to necessity and impossibility. Rather, he defines necessity and impossibility by reference to the concept of an apodictic judgment.

An apodictic judgment, according to Brentano, is a judgment that is "motivated [*motiviert*]." A judgment is motivated, he says, provided "it is immediately caused by another psychical phenomenon and we perceive this causation. An apodictic judgment is one that is motivated by the content of one's thought [*durch die Vorstellungsmaterie*]. If this kind of motivation is not present, then the judgment is said to be assertoric. Being assertoric, then, is simply a privation; such a judgment is one that is not thus motivated by the content of one's thought."[22]

In the typical case of an apodictic judgment, one considers a

19. B 100; Kemp Smith edition, 109-110.
20. B 106; Kemp Smith edition, 113.
21. For example, in a letter to G. Vailati, 26 April 1900.
22. *Die Lehre vom richtigen Urteil*, pp. 128-129.

certain compound content — say, a thing that is both round and square. The thought of this content directly causes one to reject it: one perceives that the thought of this content is the cause of the rejection of it; and the rejection is directly evident.[23] One is then said to reject the round square apodictically. And one may express this apodictic rejection by saying "Round squares are impossible." Thus Brentano says that "wherever there is apodictic evidence, there is always an evident perception of causality, and thus a compound of evident perceptions [*ein mehrfaches evidentes Wahrnehmen*]"[24]

If the thought content should directly cause one to accept the content, and if one were to perceive this causation, then the apodictic judgment would be affirmative and one could express oneself by saying that the object thought of is *necessary*. But we do not in fact make such affirmative apodictic judgments, according to Brentano, even though such affirmative apodictic judgments *could* be made. (We shall consider presently the situation under which such a judgment could be made.)

Judgments of *possibility*, as we shall see, are also apodictic judgments. Thus Brentano does not recognize Kant's category of problematic judgments. For the latter category, according to Kant, is not apodictic and yet comprises judgments of possibility and impossibility.

Some of Brentano's observations suggest that his theory of the modal judgment may be called an *expressive* theory, for it is similar to the expressive theories of ethical judgments that were defended by many philosophers in the middle of the present century. An expressive theory of ethics tells us that sentences ostensibly predicating an ethical characteristic of something (e.g., "Pleasure is intrinsically good," "Stealing is wrong") *express* certain states of mind, but do not actually assert anything about the world.

Those who held the emotive theory of ethics held that the states of mind expressed by ethical statements are neither true nor false — neither correct nor incorrect. But Brentano holds that the apodictic judgments expressed by modal statements *are* either correct or incorrect. The statements expressing such judgments may be true or false.[25]

23. See *Die Lehre vom richtigen Urteil*, p. 168.

24. *Die Abkehr vom Nichtrealen*; (Hamburg: Felix Meiner Verlag, 1966), pp. 219-220.

25. See his notes to the *Kategorienlehre*, p. 315.

According to Brentano, the sentence "Round squares are impossible" expresses an apodictic rejection of round squares. We could say that it does tell us that there *are* no round squares; but the use of the modal term "impossible" serves only to express the fact that our rejection of them is apodictic. Brentano tells us that, if we purge our language of fictions, then we will not speak of the "eternal subsistence of the impossibility of a round square." This "apparent affirmation" will be replaced by a "negative judgment, which rejects a round square apodictically."[26]

The sentence "Eternal objects, such as properties and numbers, are necessary" might also be thought to express an apodictic acceptance. In this case it would tell us that there are such things as properties and numbers, and the use of "necessary" would serve to express the fact that our acceptance of such things is apodictic.

Actually Brentano does not himself express any such apodictic acceptances. Our apodictic judgments are all negative; they are all rejections.

But when Brentano discusses St. Anselm's ontological argument and the idea of God, he suggests that, if we *could* have an adequate or complete idea of God, then the having of such an idea would cause an apodictic acceptance. "If we were to have a complete intuition of God — instead of an incomplete concept — then we could ascertain his existence: we would immediately apprehend his necessity."[27] But evidently this would be the only possible occasion for a correct affirmative apodictic judgment.[28] (Brentano's proofs that there is a necessary being do not yield necessary propositions as their conclusions. Each proof is a *reductio ad absurdum*: one premise says that there are contingent things; another says that if there were no necessary being then there would be no contingent things; and the assertoric conclusion is that there is a necessary being.)

The Modalities

Let us see if we can systematize the various suggestions that Brentano makes about the *modalia*. I will attempt to adapt his theory

26. *Kategorienlehre*, p. 20.

27. *Vom Dasein Gottes* (Hamburg: Felix Meiner 1968), p. 58.

28. At any rate, this is Kastil's interpretation. See his note 11 on page 533 of *Vom Dasein Gottes.*

to the traditional six modal concepts: impossibility, necessity, possibility, nonnecessity, contingency, and noncontingency.

Beginning with the concept of impossibility, we could say:

(M1) "A is *impossible*" expresses an apodictic rejection of A.

Necessity then could be viewed in an analogous way:

(M2) "A is *necessary*" expresses an apodictic affirmation of A.

But Brentano does not in fact provide us with such an account of necessity; for, as we have noted, he believes that the only correct apodictic judgments are negative and hence denials or rejections and not acceptances of affirmations.

But we may note that, according to Brentano, the apodictic judgments referred to in M1 and M2 may be accompanied by the following *assertoric* judgments:

(M1.1) There is a correct apodictic rejector of A.
(M2.2) There is a correct apodictic acceptor of A.

What of "possible,", as in "It is possible that there are unicorns." One who says such a thing is not telling us that there *are* any unicorns, and he would not seem to be making an apodictic judgment. Unlike Kant, Brentano does not say that there is a type of judgment which is "problematic"; hence he does not explicate possibility by reference to such judgment. Rather, he suggests that a judgment about possibility is a rejection of an apodictic judgment. "If I say that a thing is possible, I do not thereby accept or affirm a thing; what I do is to deny, of anyone who apodictically rejects the thing, that he judges correctly."[29]

Should we say, then, that "A is possible" expresses the negative judgment that there are no correct apodictic rejectors of A? This is not quite enough. Suppose I think of a certain type of perpetual motion machine and wonder whether it is possible; I am not yet ready to commit myself to the thesis that it is possible or to the thesis that it is impossible; but I feel confident that no one else has ever thought of such a machine and therefore I feel confident that it has no apodictic rejectors. In such a case, I would judge that it has no *correct* apodictic rejectors (for if it has no apodictic rejectors then it has no correct ones). Yet I am not prepared to say that the machine is possible. Hence it is one thing to judge that A has no correct apodictic rejectors; it is another thing to judge that A is possible.

29. *The True and the Evident*, p. 121; *Wahrheit und Evidenz*, p. 138.

I think we may fill in Brentano's view by saying that the "problematic" judgment, that A is possible, is actually a certain type of apodictic judgment. In saying that A is possible, I am expressing the judgment — not merely that there *are* no correct A rejectors — but that there *cannot* be any correct A rejectors. In other words:

(M3) "A is *possible*" expresses an apodictic rejection of correct apodictic A rejectors.

Kant's problematic judgment, then, becomes a type of apodictic judgment.

We may note that an assertoric judgment will be related to M3 as M1.1 and M1.2 are related to M1 and M2, respectively. A similar observation may be made with respect to the other apodictic judgments singled out below.

The modal concept of nonnecessity (which Brentano does not in fact discuss) could be treated in an analogous way:

(M4) "A is *nonnecessary*" expresses an apodictic rejection of correct apodictic A acceptors.

We are left, then with two modal concepts: contingency and noncontingency.

What is contingent is what is both possible and nonnecessary. What kind of judgment, then, is expressed by saying "A is contingent"? If one says that a certain thing is contingent, one is expressing the apodictic judgment that the thing has no correct apodictic acceptors and no correct apodictic rejectors. In other words:

(M5) "A is *contingent*" expresses an apodictic rejection of judgers who are either correct apodictic A acceptors or correct apodictic A rejectors.

What is noncontingent is what is either necessary or impossible. If we say that a thing A is noncontingent, we are, in effect, expressing an apodictic rejection of judgers who correctly judge A to be necessary or who correctly judge A to be impossible. Our judgment therefore, would seem to be somewhat complex. For it comes to this:

(M6) "A is *noncontingent*" expresses an apodictic rejection of judgers who are either (i) correct apodictic rejectors of correct apodictic A rejectors or (ii) correct apodictic rejectors of correct apodictic A acceptors.

Axioms

Although Brentano writes at length about axioms, he observes that strictly speaking there are no such *things* as axioms. Sentences ostensibly about such things are actually expressive of judgments about apodictic rejectors:

> Strictly we should not speak of the 'concept' of an axiom, for an axiom cannot be an object [*Objekt*]. This expression does not signify any *ens reale,* but we can have only *entia realia* as objects. If we say that we have an axiom as the object of our thought, then the object of our thought is actually one who judges axiomatically [*einen axiomatisch Urteilenden*]. An axiomatic judger is one who rejects a compound object, immediately, apodictically, and with evidence [*ein mit Evidenz unmittelbar apodiktisch ein zusammengesetztes Objekt Verwerfender*][30]

Some axiomatic statements purport to describe relations that obtain necessarily between *propositions.* But the statements, according to Brentano, do not commit us to the being of such entities as propositions. They may all be interpreted as expressing the apodictic rejection of certain types of judger.

Thus Brentano puts the law of contradiction this way: "It is impossible for one to deny something correctly if another accepts it correctly, i.e., with evidence; and it is also impossible for one to accept something correctly if another denies it correctly; provided that in each of the two cases the judgers think with the same mode of thinking [*mit demselben Modus des Vorstellens*] and judge with the same mode of judgment."[31] He puts the law of excluded middle in an analogous way.

It should be kept in mind that sentences ostensibly about *propositions* are all fictional according to Brentano. We should not suppose that, corresponding to the two sentences, "There are horses" and "There are no horses," there are two propositions one of which contradicts the other. One who utters the first sentence may be accepting horses and one who utters the second may be rejecting them. The two judgers will be concerned with the same object. And the word "not," instead of expressing a negative content, will express the act of rejection. This fact will make the formulation of certain

30. "Zur Axiomatic" (E L 4), 16 February 1916, paragraph 37; in *Die Lehre vom richtigen Urteil*, p. 168.

31. *Die Lehre vom richtigen Urteil*, p. 175.

propositional laws somewhat complex. But we can readily see how such laws are to be formulated.

Thus any judgment may be thought of as being directed upon a certain positive content A: the affirmative judgment will accept this content A and the negative judgment will reject it. Consider once again the relation between the I-judgment ("He judges that some A is B") and the E-judgment ("He judges that no A is B"). One normally says that the *proposition* which is the object of the A-judgment contradicts the proposition which is the object of the O-judgment. But according to Brentano's theory the two judgments have the *same* object — an A which is a B. The one who makes the affirmative judgment accepts the object and the one who makes the negative judgment rejects it.

If we use the letters "p" and "q" and the like as schemata which may be replaced by English sentences (either affirmative or negative), then we may introduce the locution "He believes that p." This will tell us either that he accepts a certain content or that he rejects it. When "p" is replaced by a complete sentence, we will be able to determine whether the judgment is affirmative or negative. Consider now the result of replacing the letter "p" by the English sentence "there are horses." Then the locution "He believes that p" will tell us that he accepts horses, and "He believes that not-p" will tell us that he rejects them. Or if "p" is replaced by "There are no horses," then "He believes that p" will tell us that he rejects horses and "He believes that not-p" will tell us that he accepts them. There is no need, therefore, to think of the double negative as signifying a special complexity in the object of judgment. "He believes that not-not-p" will tell us that he believes that p.

Now we may define propositional implication in the following way:

> p implies q =Df It is impossible both correctly to believe that p and incorrectly to believe that q.

And the following will be a definition of contradiction, thought of as a relation holding between propositions:

> p contradicts q =Df It is impossible both to believe p correctly and to believe q correctly; and it is impossible both to believe p incorrectly and to believe q incorrectly.

HOMELESS OBJECTS

Meinong introduced the expression "heimatlose Gegenstände" in *Über die Stellung der Gegenstandstheorie im System der Wissenschaften*, his apologia for the theory of objects.[1] An object is homeless, he there said in effect, if it does not fall within the subjectmatter of any of the traditional or generally accepted branches of knowledge. But I think we may find it instructive to construe the term in a slightly different way. We may think of physical things and of persons as being *concreta*, and of attributes, classes, and numbers as being *abstracta*. And we might say that a homeless object is an object that is neither a *concretum* nor an *abstractum*. Such an object would be homeless, not only because it is not covered by the usual branches of knowledge, but also because there would seem to be no place for it, either in Plato's heaven or on earth.

Looking back upon Meinong's writings, more than 50 years after his death, we are led to ask, with respect to the various types of homeless object that he proposed, "Where are they now?" I shall consider just three of them: (1) certain *intentionalia*, or objects of thought; (2) what he called "*Objektive*" and what we might call "states of affairs"; and finally (3) "incomplete objects," or objects that are not completely determinate. It is with respect to these three types of object, I think, that Meinong makes his most plausible case.

I

Certain truths, it would seem, pertain to mere *intentionalia* or objects of thought. If I happen to think of a golden mountain while not thinking of any other mountain, then the mountain I am thinking of can be said to be golden. It can also be said to be a mountain, to be

1. This work was first published by R. Voightländer in Leipzig in 1907. It is republished in Band V of the *Gesamtausgabe* of Alexius Meinong, by the Akademische Druck- u. Verlagsanstalt in Graz. The editors of the entire *Gesamtausgabe* are Rudolf Haller and Rudolf Kindinger; the editor of Band V is Roderick M. Chisholm.

something that I am thinking of, and to be nonexistent. Again, if I happen to think of a round square, then one of the objects of my thought is both round and square and therefore, according to Meinong, it is not only a nonexistent but also an impossible object. Here, then, we seem to have certain truths about objects that do not exist.

It would be unphilosophical to deny these facts at the outset. If we wish to show that Meinong is wrong, we must try to show that these truths are *not* truths about objects that do not exist. But how are we to do this?

Let us take as our paradigm "The mountain I am thinking of is golden." This true sentence *seems* to say something about an object that is only an object of my thought. Can we paraphrase it in such a way that it can be seen to be concerned only with what exists or with what Meinong would call an actual "piece of reality"?[2] The sentence speaks of me, of course, and my thoughts, and presumably my thoughts can be taken to be states of me. But the problem is that these states of me are intentional: they have objects. And it is of the essence of an intentional attitude, according to Meinong, that it may "have" an object "even though the object does not exist."[3]

It is often assumed that Russell's theory of descriptions shows us how to deal with Meinong's sentence. But it is no disparagement of Russell's great contribution to philosophy to point out that it does not apply to "The mountain I am thinking of is golden." For consider what the paraphrase would be if we were to apply Russell's theory to Meinong's sentence. We would be saying: "There exists an x such that (i) x is a mountain I am thinking of, (ii) x is golden, and (iii) for every y, y is a mountain I am thinking of, then y is identical with x." This sentence, obviously, is false. For, as we have said, the mountain I am thinking of does *not* exist. But our original sentence — "The mountain I am thinking of is golden" — is true. And therefore the paraphrase is inadequate; for if a sentence is true, then no adequate paraphrase of it will be false.

Should we consider saying, then, that when I think of a golden

2. Meinong's phrase is "ein Stück Wirklichkeit." See, for example, the second edition of *Über Annahmen* (Leipzig: Johann Ambrosius Barth, 1910), p. 43; this edition appeared as Band IV of the *Gesamtausgabe*, edited by Rudolf Haller.

3. Compare p. 382 of Band II of the *Gesamtausgabe* (1971), edited by Rudolf Haller.

mountain, then the golden mountain exists "in my mind" — just as, according to St. Anselm, when a man thinks of God, then God exists at least "in the man's understanding"? This, of course, would require us to modify to a certain extent the datum with which we began. We would have to say of the mountain I am thinking of, not that it does not exist, but rather that it does not exist "outside my mind." But can one believe that such a statement is literally true — that when I think of a mountain, then a *mountain* exists *in my mind,* that when I think of God, then *God* exists in my mind, just as there are nerves and brain cells *in my head?* If we do say this, then, as Meinong seems to recognize, we will have given St. Anselm most of what he needs to establish the conclusion of his ontological argument.[4] But this, of course, is not to say that this "in the mind" or "intentional inexistence" theory is false.

Franz Brentano who had once been inclined himself to accept this theory, saw the conclusive objection to it. "After all," he said, "a contradictory object, one that is plainly impossible, can be thought about easily enough."[5] And surely a contradictory object cannot exist anywhere — in the mind or out of it.

We should remind ourselves of just what it is that Meinong is saying about golden mountains and round squares. He is not saying that there *are* such objects or that, when we think about them, then they have a certain type of being. He is saying rather that, since we can think about these objects and say various true things about them, then they *have* certain characteristics even though they cannot be said to *be.* They have a *Sosein* even though they haven't any *Sein.* This is Meinong's doctrine of *Außersein:* certain objects which are such that there are no such objects have certain definite characteristics. Or,

4. Meinong suggests that the ontological argument can be adequately dealt with only within his theory of objects; compare *Über die Stellung der Gegenstandstheorie*, p. 18.

5. Franz Brentano, *Kategorienlehre* (Hamburg: Felix Meiner, 1968), p. 8, ed. Alfred Kastil. I discuss Brentano's earlier views on intentional inexistence in "Brentano on Descriptive Psychology and the Intentional," in Edward N. Lee and Maurice Mandelbaum, eds., *Phenomenology and Existentialism* (Baltimore: The Johns Hopkins Press, 1967), pp. 1-23; the paper may also be found in Harold Morick, ed., *Introduction to the Philosophy of Mind* (Glenview, Ill., Scott, Foresman and Company, 1970), pp. 109-149.

more briefly, from the fact that an object is *something* it does not follow that the object *is.*[6]

Let us consider, then, a slightly different approach to our sentence "The mountain I am thinking of is golden." Perhaps it can be construed as telling us, not about something which is related to me as being the *object* of my thought, but only about the *way* in which I happen to be thinking. This is the approach that suggests itself in connection with certain of Meinong's other homeless objects — in particular, those things that he called *Empfindungsgegenstände.*[7] One might say, as Meinong would, that the true sentence "I am sensing a red sensation" describes a relation between me and a certain object which has the property of being red. But one might also say this, instead: "I am sensing a red sensation" says of me, not that there is a certain *object* which I am sensing, but only that I am sensing in a certain *way* — in the way in which I might sense, for example, if I were to be stimulated by a red thing under certain optimum observation conditions. If this "adverbial" theory of sensation is correct, then we could say that "I am sensing a red sensation" only *seems* to be a statement that relates me to a certain other object. It might be rephrased, for philosophical purposes, as "I am sensing redly."

Without asking whether this "adverbial" theory is an adequate account of sensation, let us ask whether an analogous theory will hold for *intentionalia*, or objects of thought. For simplicity, let us consider unicorns for the moment, instead of the golden mountain. What are we to say if a philosopher tells us that "Jones is thinking about a unicorn" means the same as "Jones is thinking unicornically"? We should ask him, of course, what he means by his adverb "unicornically"? It will not do for him to say merely that "Jones is thinking unicornically" means the same as "Jones is thinking about a unicorn," for in this case although he may have buried our problem

6. Compare *Über emotionale Präsentation*, p. 22; this work, which first appeared in 1917, is reprinted in Band III of the *Gesamtausgabe*, edited by Rudolf Kindinger. Other references to the general doctrine of *Außersein* may be found in my paper "Beyond Being and Nonbeing," in Rudolf Haller, ed., *Jenseits von Sein und Nichtsein: Beiträge zur Meinong-Forschung,* published in Graz by the Akademische Druck- u. Verlagsanstalt 1972.

7. Compare *Uber die Stellung der Gegenstandstheorie im System der Wissenschaften*, pp. 9-14.

he will not have solved it. If the adverbial theorist really has a contribution to make, he will try to reason somewhat as follows.

"I have proposed 'Jones is thinking unicornically' as a locution which is less misleading philosophically than the original 'Jones is thinking about a unicorn.' The original sentence *seems* to relate Jones to a unicorn but actually it does not. 'Jones is thinking about a unicorn' has no more to do with a unicorn than does 'The Emperor decorated his tunic ornately.' Neither sentence has to do with unicorns, despite the fact that the word 'unicorn' may be found in each. Similarly the sentence 'Jones is thinking about a horse' has no more to do with horses than does 'The Ship's Store has a fine anchor selection.' My way of paraphrase — 'Jones is thinking unicornically' and 'Jones is thinking horsishly' — simply remove these misleading suggestions and thus enable us to escape from our pseudoproblems. In my paraphrases the words 'unicorn' and 'horse' do not function at all as such, and the adverbs 'unicornically' and 'horsishly' serve only as reminders so that we will not forget what it was we were using the sentences to say."

But our theorist is mistaken. It is not true to say that 'Jones is thinking about a unicorn' has no more to do with unicorns than does 'The Emperor decorated his tunic ornately.' Consider the premises 'Jones thinks only of things that exist' and 'Jones never thinks of things that do not exist.' If we take either of these with 'Jones is thinking about a unicorn,' then we may derive the conclusion that there *are* unicorns. Hence if our theorist's paraphrase of our original sentence is accurate, then the validity of the following inference will be preserved:

Jones thinks unicornically
Jones thinks only of things that exist
There are unicorns

But how could the inference be valid if 'Jones thinks unicornically' has no more to do with unicorns then does 'The Emperor decorated his tunic ornately'?

Many philosophers, in recent years, have attempted to explicate intentional phenomena by reference to language. Some seem to have thought that such a sentence as 'Jones is thinking about a unicorn' might be construed as relating Jones to certain linguistic expressions. Can we thus interpret the sentence linguistically? Shall we say that 'Jones is thinking about a unicorn' tells us that Jones is thinking about the *word* 'unicorn'? If Jones knows no English, he might think about a unicorn without thinking about the word 'unicorn', and he might think about the word 'unicorn', without thinking about a unicorn. Shall we say, then, that Jones is thinking about a word which, in his language, means to him what "unicorn" means to English-speaking people'? But surely one doesn't have to think of the name of a thing in order to be able to think about the thing. Otherwise, one couldn't think about the name of a thing without thinking about the name of the name of the thing, and so on *ad infinitum.* Should we assume that people who don't have any language are unable to think of things that don't exist?

Even if these difficulties can be circumvented, the linguistic theory seems to leave us with our problem. For if we are to explicate 'Jones is thinking about a unicorn' in terms of the relation of Jones to certain words, we must at some point refer to what it is that is meant by the words. More particularly, we must speak of expressions that mean unicorn. (Note that whereas '"Einhorn" means unicorn' tells us what 'Einhorn' means: '"Einhorn" means the same as "unicorn"' does not. One cannot infer the meaning of 'Einhorn' from the latter sentence unless one knows that 'unicorn' means unicorn.) How are we to paraphrase the locution 'W means unicorn' without reference to objects that do not exist?

Meinong holds quite correctly, it seems to me, that the semantic properties of a language (if we take "a language" in its ordinary sense) must be explicated by reference to the intentionality of thoughts. The 'aboutness' of words is to explicated by reference to the 'aboutness' of thoughts, rather than conversely. Thus Meinong writes:

> Everyone would concede that one and the same word can 'mean' ['*bedeuten*'] different things at different times, or in different places, or for different social groups, or for different families, or for different individuals. We may say very generally that a word always 'means' the object of the idea that it 'expresses' ['*ausdrückt*'], and conversely that it always expresses the idea of the object that it means... Actual meaning is always meaning for someone... A word has meaning only to the extent that it expresses; more exactly, a word has meaning only to the extent that it expresses an intellectual experience whose object constitutes the meaning of the word.[8]

Returning now to our original sentence, "The mountain I am thinking of is golden," let us summarize Meinong's position. It is true

8. *Über Annahme*, Second Edition, pp. 25-26.

that the mountain I am thinking of is golden; there is no plausible way of interpreting this truth other than to say that it refers to a relation between me and a golden mountain; therefore it can be truly said that a golden mountain has the property of being thought about by me; but there are no golden mountains; hence objects which are such that there are no such objects have certain attributes or properties.

Of objects which are such that there are no such objects, according to Meinong, some are *intentionalia* and some are not. (There are many truths, he believes, which hold of objects which no one will ever have thought of and which have no kind of being at all.) But even if we restrict ourselves to *intentionalia*, we may preserve a number of those distinctions which seem to be peculiar to Meinong's theory of objects. As we will see in more detail below, we can say that some objects are *complete* and others *incomplete* — a complete object, unlike an incomplete one, being an object whose *Sosein* is determinate in every respect. And we can say that some objects are *possible* and others *impossible*. If you are thinking of a golden mountain and I am thinking of a round square, then the object of your thought is a possible object (in this instance, a merely-possible object) but the object of my thought is an impossible object. An impossible object is one that has a contradictory *Sosein*: its being is precluded by the set of characteristics that it has. Once we grasp the nature of such an object, Meinong says, we see "the necessity of its non-being."[9]

We may not be entirely happy with this kind of talk. But I feel that we cannot reject it in good conscience until we have provided an alternative way of interpreting "The mountain I am thinking of is golden."

II

Objectives (*Objektive*) constitute our second class of homeless objects. The case for objectives is best seen if we consider certain other facts about intentional phenomena. More particularly, let us consider certain objects that may be common to such attitudes as believing, wondering, questioning, hoping, fearing, wishing, wanting, and striving. There are true sentences of the following sort: "I have been thinking about what it is that obsesses him"; "There is

9. *Über die Stellung*, etc., p. 76.

something we have all wished for at one time or another that only he has the courage to try to bring about"; "What Jones desires is the very thing that Robinson fears"; "There are things he believes that no other rational person would believe"; and "There is something he knows that you and I do not know." So far as I have been able to see, there is no adequate analysis of such sentences which does not presuppose that there *are* certain things which are neither *abstracta* nor *concreta* and which constitute the objects of the attitudes in question.

These objects — or objectives — are most naturally referred to by "that"-clauses; e.g., "that there will be no more wars" and "that there are ghosts." But they may also be designated by sentential gerundives: "there being no more wars" and "there being ghosts." And, as Meinong makes abundantly clear, there are many other devices in our languages for singling out such objects. "'That A exists', 'A exists', and 'The existence of A' all mean the same object; they differ with respect to the attitudes that the speaker uses them to express."[10] But the "that"-clause would seem to be the most natural device for referring to objectives.

Meinong makes the following observation about such clauses:

> So far as is known to me, linguists agree that our connective 'that' is basically nothing but a demonstrative pronoun. If one says, for example, 'I believe that what is pure harmonically may be impure melodically,' then, etymologically, at least, he is saying nothing other than 'I believe this: what is pure harmonically may be impure melodically.'[11]

But objectives do not serve merely as the objects of certain intentional attitudes.

According to Meinong, objectives are the bearers of value. Consider those things that are intrinsically good and those things that are intrinsically bad. Meinong speaks of "logical," "aesthetic," and "timological" value.[12] As I interpret him, he has in mind the value of

10. *Über Möglichkeit und Warscheinlichkeit* (Leipzig: Johann Ambrosius Barth. 1915), p. 28n. This work reappeared as Band VI of the *Gesamtausgabe*, edited by Roderick M. Chisholm.

11. *Über Annahmen*, Second Edition, p. 48.

12. See Band III of the *Gesamtausgabe*, p. 639. Compare also page 124 of Meinong's *Selbstdarstellung* in Raymund Schmidt, ed., *Die deutsche Philosophie der Gegenwart in Selbstdarstellungen*, Band I (Leipzig: Felix Meiner, 1921); this work appeared in Band VII of the *Gesamtausgabe*, edited by Rudolf Haller.

knowledge and insight, the value of beauty and fittingness, and the value that is to be found in pleasure and in the exercise of virtue. The contraries of these things are the things that are intrinsically bad: error and ignorance, ugliness and unfittingness, displeasure and pain, and the exercise of vice. Consider now the terms we have just used: "knowledge," "beauty," "fittingness,", "pleasure," "the exercise of virtue," "error," "ignorance," "ugliness," "displeasure," "pain," and "the exercise of vice." These terms do not denote individual things and, if we take them the way they are here intended, we cannot say that they designate properties or attributes. When we say, for example, that knowledge is intrinsically good, what we mean, more exactly, is that there being knowledge is intrinsically good; it is good that there are people who have knowledge, that there is someone who knows something. And when we say that pleasure is intrinsically good, what we mean, more exactly, is that there being pleasure is intrinsically good; it is good that people feel pleasure, that there are things that feel pleasure. These various bearers of value — there being knowledge, there being people who feel pleasure — are objectives.

Meinong also holds that necessity and contingency are primarily properties of objectives.[13] His view might be taken to imply that objectives constitute the subject matter of logic — and hence that they do have a home (in Meinong's sense but not ours). The term "proposition," as once used by Russell and Moore, the term "thought," or "*Gedanke*", as used by Frege, and the term "*Satz-an-sich*" as used by Bolzano, refer to objectives. Consider any principle of logic — say, the principle of propositional addition. One might put the principle loosely by saying "p implies (p or q)." But what does the principle tell us, more exactly?

Objectives entail and contradict objectives, and some objectives are compounded out of others. Thus that objective which is referred to by "Dion walking," or "Its obtaining that Dion walks," entails that objective which is referred to by "Either Dion walking or wheat being sold on the market." And to say that the one entails the other is to say that that compound objective which is the disjunction of the second with the negation of the first has the property of being necessary. The principle of propositional addition may be construed, then, as telling us this: any objective which is a disjunction of two

13. Compare *Über die Stellung*, etc., p. 25.

objectives such that one of the two objectives is itself a disjunction, one of whose disjuncts is the negation of the other objective, is an objective having the property of necessity. And analogously for the other principles of logic.

How else are we to interpret such principles? Meinong was clear that "psychologism" won't do.[14] It would hardly be accurate to the "apodictic" character of the principles of logic to interpret them as contingent generalizations about the ways in which people happen to think. We might interpret them, of course, as truths about *language*. Thus the principle of addition might be construed as telling us this: any sentence which is a disjunction of two sentences such that one of the two sentences is itself a disjunction, one of whose disjuncts is the negation of the other sentence, is a sentence that has the property of necessity. But Meinong would say, and I think correctly, that we cannot adequately interpret what it is to say of a *sentence* that it has the property of necessity unless we presuppose his doctrine of objectives.

Perhaps the most natural English term for Meinong's objectives is "state of affairs" — if we construe states of affairs in such a way that some of them (e.g., there being horses) may be said to occur or obtain and others of them (e.g., there being unicorns) may not be said to occur or obtain. (Meinong, however, had rejected Stumpf's term "*Sachverhalt*," which would seem to be pretty much the German equivalent of "state of affairs", on the ground that in its ordinary use it is restricted to those objectives that occur or obtain.[15]) I would say that there *are* states of affairs, some of which obtain and some of which do not obtain. But Meinong, with his doctrine of *Außersein,* puts the matter differently.

As we have seen, according to Meinong's doctrine, an object may have a *Sosein* without having a *Sein.* From the fact that there are truths about a certain object, it doesn't follow that the object exists or has any other kind of being, for there are truths about objects which are such that there are no such objects. And so Meinong does not say, as I have said, that there *are* states of affairs some of which obtain and some of which do not obtain. If he used the word "obtain" as I do, he would say that states of affairs, or objectives, are such that some of them obtain and some of them do not obtain. But, according

14. Compare *Über die Stellung*, etc., pp. 140-149.
15. *Über Annahmen*, Second Edition, p. 101.

to his doctrine, the only objectives which are such that there *are* such objectives are the ones that in my terminology, may be said to obtain. And he uses "is" where I have used "obtains": objectives are of two sorts, those which, like the being of horses, are such that there are those objectives, and those which, like the being of unicorns, are such that there are not those objectives.

Thus Meinong would say that, since there are horses, there is also the being of horses, as well as the being of the being of horses, the nonbeing of the nonbeing of horses, and the being of the nonbeing of the nonbeing of horses. And he would say that, since there are no unicorns, there is the nonbeing of unicorns, as well as the being of the nonbeing of unicorns, and the nonbeing of the being of unicorns.

Brentano thought that this infinite multiplication of objects is manifestly absurd. For it would seem to imply that an infinite number of nonthings — of *entia irrealia* — have existed throughout eternity. Consider, for example, the nonbeing of a carniverous horse. If we decide that there is such an object, then, according to Brentano, we must face the question whether it "is a universal having exemplifications in different places — say, one of them in Prague and another in Zürich — or whether it is itself an individual."[16] If it is itself an individual, where is it? There would seem to be no sufficient reason for assigning it to any one place rather than to another. Presumably, then, if it is an individual and is anywhere, then it is everywhere. Hence, since London is on the Thames, Brentano wrote, then "the objective, that London is on the Thames, would have to be in all places. It would follow that, although a red thing and a blue thing cannot be in the same place, the being of a red thing and the being of a blue thing do occupy the same places."[17]

Russell's attitude toward Meinong's theory — in 1918 — was very much like that of Brentano. "Time was," he wrote, "when I thought there were propositions, but it does not seem to me very plausible to say that in addition to facts there are also these curious shadowy

16. Franz Brentano, *Wahrheit und Evidenz* (Leipzig: Felix Meiner, 1962), p. 96; the quotation appears on page 86 of the English edition, *The True and the Evident* (London: Routledge and Kegan Paul, 1966). This edition of Brentano is edited by Oskar Kraus, the English edition by Roderick M. Chisholm.

17. The quotation is from a brief manuscript dictated by Brentano on January 23, 1916 and entitled "Von den sogenannten 'Objektiven'". A copy of the manuscript is on file in the Brentano Archive at Brown University.

things going about such as 'That to-day is Wednesday' when in fact it is Tuesday... To suppose that in the actual world of nature there is a whole set of false propositions going about is to my mind monstrous."[18]

Russell's misgivings, at least in the passage quoted, are concerned only with those objectives which, according to Meinong, are such that there are no such objectives — those objectives that Russell called "false propositions." Meinong might have replied on the basis of the doctrine of *Außersein.* If today is Wednesday, then, although there are truths about today being Tuesday, that objective which is today being Tuesday is such that there is no such objective. (This reply is not available to us if we say, contrary to Meinong, that there *is* such a thing as today being Tuesday and that it does not obtain. But we might well object to Russell's suggestion that today being Tuesday is something which, like a storm or an epidemic, might "go about in nature" on Wednesday.)

Brentano's objections suggest a dilemma: "If you say that objectives are *abstracta*, then you must have a view about the kinds of things that exemplify or instantiate them. How many things, if any, exemplify that objective which is there being no round squares? If you say that objectives are *concreta*, or individual things, then you must have a view about where they are. Is there being no round squares an objective which is to be found everywhere or nowhere. If it's nowhere how can you say it's a *concretum*?" The best strategy for Meinong, I would think, would be to go between the horns. The universe, he might well say, is by no means restricted to objects that are either *abstracta* or *concreta*. Perhaps that golden mountain I had been thinking of is a *concretum*. But it would be characteristic of Meinong to ask: "What if someone thinks of a golden mountain that is not a *concretum*?" And the incomplete objects, which we will discuss below, would also seem to be such that they are neither abstract nor concrete.

Both Russell and Brentano assume that all those truths that are taken by Meinong to be truths about objectives can be paraphrased in such a way that they can be shown not to involve such objects. Many such truths, of course, can be so paraphrased. But what of that

18. Bertrand Russell, *Logic and Knowledge* (London: George Allen and Unwin, Ltd., 1956), p. 223; the quotation is from the lectures, "The Philosophy of Logical Atomism," which Russell gave in 1918.

expressed by "There is something Jones is trying to bring about which, Smith believes, will never obtain?" If we consider just what it is that such a true sentence tells us, and if we take care not to read more or less into its meaning than is actually there, we will find, if I am not mistaken, that neither Brentano nor Russell nor any other philosopher has shown us how to interpret it without reference to those objects that Meinong called "objectives".

III

We turn, finally to objects that are incomplete *(unvollständige Gegenstande).* An object is incomplete, according to Meinong, if its *Sosein* is not completely determinate — if, say, it has a color without having any determinate color. No object that exists or has any other kind of being is indeterminate. But there are many truths about incomplete or indeterminate objects and these truths, according to Meinong, are of considerable philosophical importance.

If we countenance such *intentionalia* as the golden mountain that Mr. Jones was thinking about a while ago, then we must concede that such objects are not likely to be completely determinate. Thus the mountain Mr. Jones was thinking about may have been over 3,000 feet high and less that 40,000 feet high and yet may not have been of any particular height between those who extremes. But Meinong's theory of incomplete objects does not depend upon his theory of *intentionalia*.

Let us recall some of the traditional ways of looking upon the problems of universals. The ideal bed that Plato discusses in Book X of *The Republic* is not an attribute or property. It *is* a bed and, according to Plato, there is only *one* such bed. Since in nature this ideal bed can be imitated equally by five-foot beds, six-foot-beds, and seven-foot beds, then the presumption would seem to be that, according to Plato's doctrine, the ideal bed, although it has the property of being a bed and of having some length, does not have the property of being exactly six-feet long, or of being more than six feet long, or of being less than six feet long.[19]

According to the view of William of Champeaux, or at least

19. The Republic, Book X, 596-597; compare the interpretation in John Burnet, *Greek Philosophy: Thales to Plato* (London: Macmillan, 1928), p. 318.

according to one plausible interpretation of the view of William of Champeaux, this incompletely determined bed exists *in* every actual bed, just as the abstract object triangle (note we say "triangle" and not "triangularity") exists in determinate triangles, and just as the species man ("man" not "humanity") exists in each particular man.[20]

The object of what Locke calls "the general idea of a triangle," if such an idea *has* an object, would be incompletely determined, "for it must be neither oblique nor rectangle, neither equilateral, equicrural, nor scalene."[21] And, according to one plausible view of what Aristotle called "secondary substances," these things too, are incompletely determined objects. The secondary substance man is not an attribute or a class. Like particular men, and unlike any attribute or class, it has the property of being rational and of being a featherless biped. But it does not have the property of being six feet tall, or less than six feet tall, or more than six feet tall.[22]

We are readily led to such incompletely determined objects, Meinong suggests, if we consider that things may be truly said about *the triangle as such* and about *man as such*. Thus he writes: "The triangle is as such neither equilateral nor equiangular, neither right-angled nor oblique, nor the contrary of any of these. In such respects as well as in many others it is simply indeterminate [*unbestimmt*]."[23] And he could equally well have said that man as such is rational, but is neither Greek, nor Roman, nor Ethiopian, nor of any other race or nationality.

Meinong also holds — and here his view is remarkably like the one attributed to William of Champeaux — that every actual object is made up, in part at least, of such incompletely determined objects. Thus he says that the incomplete billiard ball, that object which is the billiard ball as such, exists in every particular billiard ball. To be sure, he adds, no one of the actual, complete billiard balls has the incomplete one as a *part*; for the incomplete billiard ball "would have to lose its incompleteness if it were to become a part of the complete

20. This was Brentano's interpretation of William of Champeaux; compare *Kategorienlehre*, p. 33.

21. *Essay concerning Human Understanding*, Book IV, Chapter 7, Section 9.

22. Compare J.N. Findlay, *Meinong's Theory of Objects and Values* (Oxford: The Clarendon Press, 1963), pp. 164-165.

23. *Über Möglichkeit und Wahrscheinlichkeit*, p. 178.

billiard ball."[24] But the incomplete one is involved or "implicated" ("*implektiert*") in each complete one.

It is not at all easy to say what Meinong here means by "implicated." But we can at least suggest *why* it was that he wanted to say that the incomplete object is thus intimately involved in the complete ones. He was concerned with the problem of what seem to be unactualized possibilities.

Consider any actual object that happens to be familiar — say, the table in this room. Being an actual object, the table is completely determined with respect to its *Sosein*, past, present, and future. Yet it may be that we can truly say "Possibly this table will stand by that window tomorrow, and possibly, too, it will not stand by that window tomorrow." Our true sentence seems to leave open two incompatible possibilities for the table. But so far as actual objects are concerned, Meinong would seem to be a Megaric.[25] He says that, with respect to the actual table that is in this room, one of the two possibilities mentioned in our true sentence is excluded. How, then, are we to interpret our true sentence?

Meinong's view seems to be that, strictly speaking, the possibility sentence is concerned, not with that object which is the actual table in this room, but with that object which is *the table in this room as we now know it.* One can say, of the table as we now know it, what one cannot say of the actual table, that it is in many respects incompletely determined.[26]

Meinong also gives us this example: "Suppose I say, of my acquaintance N, that tomorrow he could arrive at a certain place O, but also he could have arrived there yesterday instead. In saying this I have no doubt at all but that in fact the day of his arrival will be either tomorrow or not tomorrow; and I am entirely convinced either that he did actually arrive yesterday or that he did not actually arrive yesterday... If I say, then, that N has this or that possibility, then, if I am not to fall into error, I must be clear about the fact that this is not a 'having' in the strict sense of the term — not the kind of having that goes with ordinary predication."[27] Here again what Meinong seems to be getting at is that, although his acquaintance N is completely

24. Ibid., p. 211.
25. Cf. ibid., p. 223.
26. Cf. ibid., pp. 221-231.
27. Ibid., pp. 225-226.

determined, that object which is *N as Meinong knows him now* is not completely determined.

Perhaps the following summary is adequate to Meinong's reasoning and gives us a kind of argument in behalf of his incompletely determined objects. (i) One can truly say, ostensibly with respect to certain actual objects, that some of their possibilities are now open. Thus one may truly say "*a* may be F" and also "*a* may be non-F." But (ii) every actual object is completely determined. Therefore (iii) the possibility-determinations "may be F" and "may be non-F" do not *both* apply to any actual object. But (iv) there is some object to which they both apply. And (v) the most plausible suggestion as to what that something is, is that it is a certain incomplete object — say, that object which is *a* as it is now known to us.

I am not suggesting that this is a *good* argument. It is not difficult to see that there are many possible ways of escaping the conclusion. And, even if we can accept the argument, we will be left with the difficult problem of determining just how it is that that incomplete object which is *a* as we know it is related to the actual *a* which is completely determined.

Nevertheless, in evaluating Meinong's theory, one should consider just what the alternatives are. According to the alternative theory of possibility that is now held by many philosophers and logicans, what we mean when we say, "This table could be by that window tomorrow" is to be explicated in some such way as this: "Of those possible words that include all the propositions (objectives) that we know to be true of the actual world, some are such that, in them, this table will stand by that window tomorrow." But what does it mean to say that there *are* certain possible worlds which are such that, *in them, this* table stands by *that* window *tomorrow*? I am not convinced that this view is any clearer than Meinong's theory of incompletely determined objects.

BEYOND BEING AND NONBEING*

> ". . . das Universum in der Gesamtheit des Wirklichen noch lange nicht erschöpf ist." Meinong

Meinong wrote: "There are objects of which it is true that there are no such objects."[1] But he was well aware that this statement of his doctrine of *Außersein* was needlessly paradoxical. Other statements were: "The non-real" is not "a mere nothing" and "The object as such . . . stands 'beyond being and non-being'."[2] Perhaps the clearest statement was provided by Meinong's follower, Ernst Mally: *"Sosein is independent of Sein."*[3] We could paraphrase Mally's statement by saying:"An object may have a set of characteristics whether or not it exists and whether or not it has any other kind of being."

It is commonly supposed that this doctrine of *Außersein* is absurd and that whatever grounds Meinong may have had for affirming it were demolished by Russell's theory of descriptions. I believe,

* I wish to express my indebtedness to the late Dr. Rudolf Kindinger. Certain portions of this paper are adapted from my "Jenseits von Sein und Nichtsein", in *Dichtung und Deutung: Gedächtnisschrift für Hans M. Wolff,* edited by Karl S. Guthke, Bern-Munich: Francke Verlag 1961.

1. A. Meinong, "Über Gegenstandstheorie," *Gesammelte Abhandlungen* Leipzig: Johann Ambrosius Barth 1929, *Meinong Gesamtausgabe*, Graz: Akademische Druck- und Verlagsanstalt 1971, Vol. II, p. 490. This work first appeared in 1904, in the collection *Untersuchungen zur Gegenstandstheorie und Psychologie,* Leipzig: Johann Ambrosius Barth, edited by Meinong. It is translated as "The theory of Objects," in *Realism and the Background of Phenomenology*, Glencoe, III., The Free Press 1960, edited by Roderick M. Chisholm; the quotation above appears on page 83.

2. *Gesammelte Abhandlungen,* Vol. II, pp. 486, 494; English translation in *Realism and the Background of Phenomenology,* pp. 79, 86.

3. "Untersuchungen zur Gegenstandstheorie des Messens", in *Untersuchungen zur Gegenstandstheorie und Psychologie,* pp. 51-120; the quotation may be found on page 127.

however, that this supposition is false. I shall attempt here to set forth the doctrine in its most extreme form and I shall then consider what may be said in its favour.

I.

The fundamental theses of Meinong's theory of objects are (1) that there are objects which do not exist and (2) that objects which are such that there are *no* such objects are nonetheless constituted in some way or other and thus may be made the subject of true predication. The second of these two theses is the doctrine of *Außersein.* The first thesis, as Meinong says, is familair to traditional metaphysics. But traditional metaphysics, he adds, has had "a prejudice in favor of the actual."[4] Though it has had a proper concern for "ideal objects," those things that merely subsist *(bestehen)* and do not exist, it has neglected those things that have no being at all. Hence the need for a more encompassing theory of objects.

Among the characteristic tenets of the theory of objects are the following.

Of objects, some exist and others do not exist. Thus horses are included among objects that exist, and unicorns and golden mountains are included among objects that do not exist.

Of objects that do not exist, some may yet be said to be, or to subsist, and others may not be said to be at all.

Thus if existence is thought of as implying a spatio-temporal locus, then there are certain ideal objects that do not exist. Among these are properties or attributes and the objects of mathematics, as well as states of affairs (what Meinong calls "*Objektive*"). Since there are horses, for example, there is also the being of horses, the being of the being of horses, the nonbeing of the nonbeing of horses, and the being of the nonbeing of the nonbeing of horses. And since there are no unicorns, there is also the nonbeing of unicorns, the being of the nonbeing of unicorns, the nonbeing of the being of unicorns, and the nonbeing of the nonbeing of unicorns.[5]

4. *Gesammelte Abhandlungen,* Vol. II, p. 485; English translation, p. 78

5. See *Gesammelte Abhandlungen,* Vol. II, pp. 486-8; English translation, pp. 79-80. The most complete statement of Meinong's theory of states of affairs, or *Objektive,* may be found in Chapter III ("Das Objektiv") of *Über Annahmen*, Second Edition, Leipzig: Johann Ambrosius Barth 1910.

But, though every object may correctly be said to be something or other, it is not the case that every object may correctly be said to be.[6] Unicorns, golden mountains, and round squares may not be said to be at all. Everything, however, *is* an object, whether or not it exists or has any other kind of being, and indeed whether or not it is even thinkable. (Whatever is unthinkable, after all, at least has the property of *being* unthinkable.) And every object, clearly, has the characteristics it does have whether or not it has any kind of being. This last is the proposition Mally expressed by saying that the *Sosein* of an object is independent of its *Sein*.

The theory of *Außersein* therefore, should be distinguished both from Platonism, as this term is currently interpreted, and from the reism, or concretism, of Brentano and Kotarbinski. Thus the Platonist might be said to reason as follows: "(P) Certain objects that do not exist have certain properties; but (Q) an object has properties if and only it is real; hence (R) there are real objects that do not exist." The reist, on the other hand, reasons from not-R and Q to not-P; that is to say, he takes as his premises Plato's second premise and the contradictory of Plato's conclusion and then derives the contradictory of Plato's first premise. But Meinong, like Plato and unlike the reist, accepts P as well as R; unlike both Plato and the reist, he rejects Q; and then *he* derives a conclusion that is unacceptable both to the Platonist and to the reist - namely, "(S) The totality of objects extends far beyond the confines of what is merely real."[7]

Once this conclusion is accepted, a number of interesting distinctions may be made. These would seem to be peculiar to Meinong's theory of objects.

Thus objects may be subdivided into those which are possible and those which are impossible. (We should note, incidentally, that to say of an object that it is only a possible object is *not* to say of it that it is only possibly an object. For possible objects, as well as impossible objects, *are* objects.) Possible objects, unlike impossible objects, have

6. "Jeder Gegenstand ist *etwas,* aber nicht jedes Etwas *ist*." Mally, op. cit., p. 126.

7. Compare the quotation at the head of this article; the quotation is from Meinong's posthunous *Zur Grundlegung der allgemeinen Werttheorie*, Graz: Leuschner & Lubensky 1923, edited by Ernst Mally, p. 158; Meinong Gesamtausgabe, Graz: Akademische Druck- u. Verlagsanstalt 1968, Vol. III, p. 638.

noncontradictory *Soseins*. Golden mountains, for example, although they have no kind of being, may be possible objects; for the *Sosein* of a golden mountain need not preclude its *Sein*. But some golden mountains are impossible objects — for example, those that are both golden and nongolden, and those that are both round and square. An impossible object is thus an object with a contradictory *Sosein* — a *Sosein* that precludes its object's *Sein*.[8]

Soseins, too, are objects and therefore every *Sosein* has a *Sosein*. An object which is not itself a *Sosein* is an impossible object if it *has* a contradictory *Sosein*. May a *Sosein*, too, be an impossible object? Mally answers this question in a remarkable paragraph which may be paraphrased as follows:

"Like any other object a *Sosein* is an impossible object if *it* has a *Sosein* which precludes its *Sein*; that is to say, a *Sosein* is an impossible object if its own *Sosein* is contradictory. A *Sosein* would have a contradictory *Sosein* if it had the property of being the *Sosein* of an object which does *not* have that *Sosein*. The circularity of a possible square is thus an impossible *Sosein*. For the circularity of a possible square has itself a contradictory *Sosein*: that of being the circularity of something that isn't circular. But an impossible *Sosein* is not the same as a contradictory *Sosein*. The circularity of a possible square must be distinguished from the circularity (and squareness) of a *round* square; the former is an impossible *Sosein*, but the latter is not. The circularity of a round square is a contradictory *Sosein* but *not* an impossible *Sosein*. What is impossible is that there be an object that is both round and square. But it is *not* impossible that a round square be both round and square. Indeed, it is *necessary* that a round square be both round and square."[9]

Objects may also be classified as being either complete or incomplete. Where an impossible object is an object having a *Sosein*

8. Once we grasp the nature of an impossible object, according to Meinong, we become aware of "the necessity of its nonbeing." Meinong does not use the expression "necessary object", but he says, with respect to abstract objects, that once we grasp *their* nature, we become aware of "the necessity of their being". See *Über die Stellung der Gegenstandstheorie im System der Wissenschaften*, Leipzig: R. Voitländer Verlag, 1970, p. 76.

9. Paraphrased from Ernst Mally, *op. cit.*, pp. 128-9. I have translated *"Viereck"* as "square", have added italics, and have written "possible square" in two places where Mally wrote only *"Viereck"*,

that violates the law of contradiction, an *incomplete object* is one having a *Sosein* that violates the law of excluded middle. Of the round squares that were being contemplated just now, it may be neither true nor false to say of the one that was contemplated by you that it is larger than the one that was contemplated by me.[10]

Of all objects, the most poorly endowed would seem to be what Meinong calls *defective objects*. Indeed, they are so poorly endowed that Meinong seems to be uncertain as to whether they are objects at all. If I wish that your wish will come true, then the object of my wish is whatever it is that you happen to wish. And if, unknown to me, *your* wish is that my wish will come true, then the object of your wish is what it is that I happen to wish. But this object, in the circumstances imagined, would seem to have very little *Sosein* beyond that of being our mutual object. Meinong felt, incidentally, that this concept of a defective object might be used to throw light upon the logical paradoxes.[11]

It is a mistake, then, to express the doctrine of *Außersein* by saying that, according to Meinong, such objects as golden mountains and round squares have a kind of being other than existence or subsistence. Meinong's point is that they have no kind of being at all. They are "homeless objects", not even to be found in Plato's heaven.[12]

Why assume, then, that an object may have a *Sosein* and yet no *Sein* — that an object may have a set of characteristics and yet no kind of being at all?

10. On incomplete objects, see Meinong's *Über Möglichkeit und Wahrscheinlichkeit,* Leipzig: Johann Ambrosius Barth 1915, pp. 179-180, also *Über die Stellung der Gegenstandstheorie im System der Wissenschaften,* pp. 118-123.

11. Meinong discusses defective objects, in *Über emotionale Präsentation,* Vienna: Alfred Hölder, 1917, pp. 10-26; *Meinong Gesamtausgabe*, Graz: Akademische Druck-u. Verlagsanstalt 1968, Vol. III, pp. 294-310.

12. See *Über die Stellung der Gegenstandstheorie im System der Wissenschaften,* Section One ("Heimatlose Gegenstände"), p. 8 ff. In the *Introduction to Mathematical Philosophy*, London: George Allen & Unwin, Ltd. 1919, Russell said that, according to Meinong, such objects as the golden mountain and the round square "must have some kind of logical being" (p.169). But in "On Denoting" and in his earlier writings on Meinong, he does not make this mistake.

II.

The prima facie case for this doctrine of *Außersein* lies in the fact that there are many truths which *seem*, at least, to pertain to objects which are such that there are no such objects. It is reasonable to assume that this prima facie case would be weakened if we could show, with respect to these truths, that they need not be construed as pertaining to these homeless objects. It is also reasonable to assume, I think, that Meinong's case will be strengthened to the extent that we find ourselves *unable* to show, with respect to any one of these truths, that it need not be construed as pertaining to such objects.

There are at least five groups of such truths that have been singled out in recent literature. (The groups are not mutually exclusive and they may not be exhaustive.) For there would seem to be at least five different sorts of things that we may say of an object that does not exist or have any other kind of being: (1) we may say that the object does not exist; (2) we may say what the object is without implying either that it exists or that it does not exist; (3) we may note what expressions in our language are used to refer to that object; (4) we may say that the object is involved in myth or fiction and that, as so involved, it is richly endowed with attributes; or (5) we may say that someone's intentional attitude is directed upon that object.

Meinong's best case, I think, lies with the final group — with those truths that seem to pertain to the nonexistent objects of our intentional attitudes. But let us consider them all in as favourable a light as we can.

(1) Examples of the first group are "Things that are both round and square do not exist" and "Unicorns do not exist." Can we paraphrase these in such a way that they may be seen to involve no reference to nonexistent objects? The first example presents fewer problems than the second, but it is doubtful that we can paraphrase it in a way that would satisfy Meinong.

The obvious paraphrase of "Things that are both round and square do not exist" would be "Everything that does exist is such that it is not both round and square." But, Meinong would say, where the subject-term of the paraphrase may be taken to refer to any piece of reality one chooses, the subject-term of the original is intended to refer to "what does not exist and is therefore not a piece of reality at all."[13]

13. *Über die Stellung der Gegenstandstheorie im System der Wissen-*

The obvious paraphrase of "Unicorns do not exist" would be "Everything that does exist is such that it is not a unicorn." But this, Meinong could say, leaves us with a reference to nonexistent objects. To say of a thing that is not a unicorn is to say of it that it is not identical with any unicorn; and to say of a thing that it is not identical with any unicorn is to relate it to objects that do not exist.

Hence we may wish to replace "a unicorn", in "Everything that does exist is such that it is not a unicorn", by certain predicates. But what predicates, and how do we decide? Let us suppose (to oversimplify somewhat) that we are satisfied with "single-horned" and "equine." Then we paraphrase "Unicorns do not exist" as "Everything that does exist is such that it is not both single-horned and equine". Meinong may now repeat the objection he had made to our attempted paraphrase of the first example above. And he may add still another.

How did we happen to choose the particular predicates "single-horned" and "equine"? We chose them, Meinong would say, because we know, *a priori,* that all and only unicorns are both single-horned and equine. And this *a priori* statement — "All and only unicorns are both equine and single-horned" — is one in which, once again, we have a subject-term that refers, or purports to refer, to non-existent objects. This statement, however, belongs to the second group and not to the first.

(2) Meinong writes: "If one judges that a perpetual motion machine does not exist, then it is clear that the object whose existence he is denying must have certain properties and indeed certain characteristic properties. Otherwise the judgement that the object does not exist would have neither sense nor justification."[14] Applying a similar observation to our previous example, we may say, of the judgement that unicorns do not exist, that it presupposes that unicorns are both single-horned and equine. "Unicorns are both single-horned and equine" may also be expressed as "Every existing thing is such that if it were a unicorn then it would be both equine

schaften, p. 38. Meinong's remarks were directed toward the distinction between "Ghosts do not exist *(Gespenster existieren nicht)*" and "No real thing is ghostly *(Kein Wirkliches ist Gespenst)*". Compare Richard L. Cartwright, "Negative Existentials," *Journal of Philosophy,* Vol. LVII (1960), pp. 629-639

14. *Über Annahmen,* p. 79.

and single-horned." But the presence of "a unicorn" in the latter sentence, as we have noted, enables Meinong to say that the sentence does tell us something about unicorns — namely, that if any existing thing were indentical with any one of them, then that thing would be both equine and single-horned.[15]

These truths about nonexistent objects which are presupposed, whenever we say of anything that it does not exist, are *a priori,* according to Meinong. Much of what we know about objects, he says, is thus *"daseinsfrei."*[16]

There are some *a priori* statements, according to Meinong, in which nonexistent objects are singled out by means of definite descriptions. "Not only is the much heralded gold mountain made of gold, but the round square is as surely round as it is square.[17]" What are we to say of "The golden mountain is golden"? According to Russell's theory of descriptions, some sentences of the form "The

15. By confusing use and mention, one may try to render "Unicorns are both single-horned and equine" into a statement which mentions only words. (Such a statement as "The word 'unicorn' refers to things that are both single-horned and equine" belongs to our third group, below).

16. A considerable part of Mienong's *Über die Stellung der Gegenstandstheorie im System der Wissenschaften* is devoted to *"Daseinsfreiheit"* and *"Apriorität."*

17. English translation of "The theory of Objects," page 82; *Gesammelte Abhandlungen,* Vol. II, p. 490. Russell said that if "The round square is round" is true, then "The existent round square is existent" is also true; and the latter statement, he pointed out, implies that there is a round square; see his review of *Untersuchungen zur Gegenstandstheorie und Psychologie, Mind,* Vol. XIV (1905), pp. 530-538, esp. p. 533. Meinong replied that "existent" is not a predicate, not a *"Soseinsbestimmung",* and hence he should have said that "The existent round square is existent" is false. Unfortunely, however, he attempted to draw a distinction between "is existent" and "exists" and then said that although the existent round square is existent it does not exist. See *Über die Stellung der Gegenstandstheorie im System der Wissenschaften,* pp. 16-19. Reviewing the latter work, Russell replied: "I must confess that I see no difference between existing and being existent; and beyond this I have no more to say"; *Mind,* Vol. XVI (1907), pp. 436-439, esp. p. 439. Meinong also had difficulties with "The possible round square is possible"; see *Über Möglichkeit und Wahrscheinlichkeit,* pp. 277-289. What he should have said, I think, is that "possible" is not a predicate, not a *"Soseinsbestimmung,"* and hence that "The possible round square is possible" is false.

thing which is F is G" may be paraphrased into sentences of the following form: "There exists an x such that x is F and x is G, and for every (existing) y, if y is F then y is identical with x." Hence if we paraphrase "The golden mountain is golden" in this way, we will have: "There exists an x such that x is both golden and a mountain, and x is golden, and, for every (existing) y, if y is both golden and a mountain then y is identical with x." The resulting sentence would seem to refer only to objects that do exist. But is it an adequate paraphrase?

"The golden mountain is golden," according to Meinong, is *true*. But Russell's paraphrase implies "There exists an x such that x is both golden and a mountain" and is therefore *false*. How can a false statement be an adequate paraphrase of a true one?

Russell, of course, would say that Meinong is mistaken in insisting that "The golden mountain is golden" is true. But how are we to decide who is right, without begging the basic question that is involved?

(3) Semantical statements may seem to provide another type of reference to objects that do not exist or to objects such that there are no such objects. For example, "The word *'Einhorn'* in German designates unicorns"; or "The word *'Einhorn'* in German purports to designate unicorns"; or "The word *'Einhorn'* is used in German ostensibly to designate unicorns". And analogously for the word "unicorn" and its use in English. But Meinong would say — quite correctly, it seems to me — that semantical statements are really a subclass of intentional statements, statements about psychological attitudes and their objects, and hence that they belong to our fifth group below. To say that *"Einhorn"* is used to designate unicorns, according to Meinong, is to say that *"Einhorn"* is used to express those thoughts and other intentional attitudes that take unicorns as their object.[18]

(4) Statements about objects of fiction and mythology are sometimes taken as paradigm cases of statements about nonexistent objects. Examples are "Sam Weller was Mr. Pickwick's servant" and "Sam Weller was a fictitious character who didn't really exist." But if I am not mistaken, these belong with our intentional statements, below. Thus the first example, as it would ordinarily be intended,

18. See *Über Annahmen,* Second Edition, p. 26.

pertains to one of the objects of a certain story (if we take "story" in the widest sense of the word). But to say of a thing that it is an object of a certain story is to say either that someone has told a story about that thing or that someone has thought of a story about that thing. And to say that someone has told a story, or that someone has thought of a story, is to make an intentional statement. When we say "Sam Weller was a fictitious character who didn't really exist", we are not only making an intentional statement, about an object of someone's story, but we are also making a statement that belongs to our first group above — a statement saying that the object does not exist. Statements about the object of mythology are analogous, except that it may be necessary to add, again intentionally, that the story in question is one that someone believes.

(5) Meinong's best case, then, would seem to lie with those true *intentional* statements that seem to pertain to objects that do not exist. I shall distinguish four types of such statements.

The first type is exemplified by

(a) John fears a ghost.

Here we seem to have a straightforward affirmation of a relation between John and a nonexistent object. It is of the essence of an intentional attitude, according to Meinong, that it may thus "have" an object "even though the object does not exist."[19] Can we paraphrase our statement (a) in such a way that the result can be seen to involve no such apparent reference to a nonexistent object? So far as I have been able to see, we cannot. (It is true, of course, that philosophers often invent new terms and then profess to be able to express what is intended by such statements as "John fears a ghost" in their own technical vocabularies. But when they try to convey to us what their technical terms are supposed to mean, then they, too, refer to nonexistent objects such as unicorns).

It is sometimes said that Meinong did not properly understand the use of words in intentional contexts — or, in the terms of our example, that he did not properly understand the use of the expression "a ghost" in such a sentence as "John fears a ghost." He mistakenly supposed, it is suggested, that the word "ghost" has a *referential* use in "John fears a ghost." But just what was the mistake that Meinong made? He did not make the mistake of supposing that

19. See *Gesammelte Abhandlungen,* Vol. II, p. 383.

the word "ghost" in "John fears a ghost" is used to refer to something that exists or to something that is real. Is it that the word has a certain nonreferential use in such sentences and that Meinong was not aware of this use? But what *is* that nonreferential use — other than that of being used to tell us that John fears a ghost? I know of four positive suggestions, but they all seem to leave Meinong untouched. Thus it has been said (i) that the word "ghost", in "John fears a ghost", is used, not to describe the object of John's fears, but only to contribute to the description of John himself. This was essentially Brentano's suggestion.[20] But just *how* does "ghost" here contribute to the description of John? It isn't being used to tell us that *John* is a ghost, or that John's *thought* is a ghost, for these things are false, but "John fears a ghost," we may suppose, is true. Surely the only way in which the word "ghost" here contributes to the description of John is by telling us *what* the object is that he fears. It has also been suggested (ii) that the word "ghost", in "John fears a ghost," functions only as part of the longer expression "fears a ghost" and that its use in such contexts has no connection at all with the use it has in such sentences as "There is a ghost." (Compare the use of "unicorn" in "The Emperor decorated his tunic ornately.") That this suggestion is false, however, may be seen by noting that "John fears a ghost" and "John's fears are directed only upon things that really exist" together imply "There is a ghost." It has also been suggested (iii) that the word "ghost," in "John fears a ghost," is used to refer to what in other uses would constitute the sense or connotation of "ghost."[21] In this case, "John fears a ghost" would be construed as telling us that there is a certain relation holding between John and a certain set of attributes or properties. But what attributes or properties, and what relation? John himself may remind us at this point that what he fears is a certain *concretum* and not a set of attributes or properties. It has even been suggested (iv) that the word "ghost," in "John fears a ghost," is being used, in "the material

20. See Franz Brentano, *The True and the Evident*, London: Routledge Kegan Paul, 1966, English edition edited by Roderick M. Chisholm, pp. 68-69.

21. This interpretation may be suggested by Frege's "Über Sinn und Bedeutung," *Zeitschrift für Philosophie und philosophische Kritik,* Vol. C (1892), pp. 25-50; translated as "On Sense and Nomination," in *Readings in Philosophical Analysis*, New York: Appleton-Century-Crofts, Inc. 1949, edited by Herbert Feigl and Wilfrid Sellars, pp. 85-102.

mode," to refer to itself.[22] But John, of course, may not fear the *word* "ghost." What, then, would "John fears a ghost" be used to tell us about John and the word "ghost"?

The second type of intentional statement is exemplified by

(b) The mountain I am thinking of is golden.

To supply a context for such a statement, we imagine a game in which the participants are told to contemplate a mountain, such as might be found in Atlantis, and are then asked to describe the mountain they have contemplated. Meinong's "The golden mountain is golden", of our second group above, may well leave us speechless, but surely "The mountain I am thinking of is golden" may express a proposition that is true.

Russell's theory of descriptions does not provide us with a way of paraphrasing the statement, for, once again, Russell's procedure would provide us with a statement that is *false* ("There exists an x such that x is a mountain I am thinking of and x is golden, and, for every y, if y is a mountain I am thinking of, then y is identical with x").[23]

22. Carnap once suggested that "Charles thinks (asserts, believes, wonders about) A", where "A" is thought of as being the abbreviation of some sentence, may be translated as "Charles thinks 'A' "; *The Logical Syntax of Language,* New York: Harcourt, Brace and Company 1937, p. 248.

23. In "On Denoting" Russell said that "the chief objection" to Meinong's nonexistent objects "is that such objects, admittedly, are apt to infringe the law of contradiction"; see Bertrand Russell, *Logic and Knowledge,* London: George Allen and Unwin 1956, p. 45. Thus the round square that I am thinking of may be an object that is both round and nonround. Meinong's reply was that the law of contradiction (in the form, "For any attribute F, there is nothing that exemplifies F and also does not exemplify F") applies only to what is real or possible; one could hardly expect it to apply to impossible objects such as the round square. See *Über die Stellung der Gegenstandstheorie im System der Wissenschaften,* p. 16. One may also argue that certain possible objects would seem to infringe upon other logical laws. Suppose Jones, who mistakenly believes that F.D.R. was assassinated, tells us that the man he is now thinking about is the assassin of F.D.R.; from Jones' true statement it follows that the man he is thinking about murdered F.D.R.; but for any x and y, if x murdered y, then y was murdered by x; hence F.D.R. *was* murdered — and by a nonexistent object! See James Mish'alani, "Thought and Object," *The Philosophical Review,* Vol. LXXI (1962), pp. 185-201. Meinong's reply could be: The statement "For any x

The participants in the game we have imagined may well compare mountains: "The mountain you are thinking of differs in interesting respects from the mountain I am thinking of." May we also say that the nonexistent object of one man's intentional attitude is *identical with* the nonexistent object of another man's intentional attitude? I think that we may often assume that this is the case. Such an identity statement provides us with our third example of a Meinongian intentional statement. Thus we may be agnostic and yet affirm

(c) All Mohammedans worship the same God.

But this example, I think, is more problematic than the others. If the statement in question were true, we could say, of any two Mohammedans, that the God that is worshipped by the one is identical with the God that is worshipped by the other. But can we really say this if, as we are also inclined to say, "the God that is worshipped by Mohammedans does not exist." Shouldn't we say, at most, that for any two Mohammedans, x and y, the God that x worships is *very much like* the God that y worships.[24] (And instead of saying "The

and y, if x murdered y, then y was murdered by x" is true only if our variables range over objects that exist; and, more generally, from the fact that it is a part of the *Sosein* of a nonexistent object x that x stands in a certain relation R to an existent object y, it does not follow that it is a part of the *Sosein* of y either that y is related by the converse of R to x or that x related by R to y.

24. P.T. Geach cites this example: "Hob thinks a witch has blighted Bob's mare, and Nob wonders whether she (the same witch) killed Cob's sow"; in "Intentional Identity", *Journal of Philosophy,* Vol. LXIV (1967), pp. 627-632. There is a certain ambiguity in the example, for it may be taken to imply either that the object of Hob's thought, is identical with the object of Nob's wondering or only that Nob *thinks* that it is. Taking it in its first sense, how could we ever find out that it is true? Hob may assure us that he thinks there is one and only one witch who blighted Bob's mare and that he also thinks that that witch is F,G,H, and. . . (where 'F', 'G', and 'H' may be thought of as abbreviating certain predicates); and Nob may assure us that he, too, thinks there is one and only one witch who blighted Bob's mare, that that witch is F, G, H, and . . ., and also, perhaps, that he, Nob, thinks that that witch is the same as the one that Hob believes to have blighted Bob's mare. But our statement of these facts does not entail that the object of Hob's thought is identical with the object of Nob's wondering. And, given that there are no witches, it is difficult to think of anything we could learn from Hob and Nob that would entail it.

God that is worshipped by Mohammedans does not exist," we might express ourselves more accurately by saying "Every Mohammedan is such that the God that he worships does not exist.") But for Meinong's purpose, of course, it is enough to say that one nonexistent object is "very much like" another.

If we can never be sure that the nonexistent object upon with one man's intentional attitude is directed is identical with the nonexistent object upon which another man's intentional attitude is directed, we can be sure, on occasion, that the nonexistent object upon which one of a certain man's intentional attitudes is directed is identical with a nonexistent object upon which another one of that same man's intentional attitudes is directed. Thus we may say of an obsessed believer:

(d) The thing he fears the most is the same as the thing he loves the most.

Any adequate theory of the emotions would seem to imply that a man may have at any particular time a great variety of attitudes and feelings all directed upon a single object — even thought that object does not exist[25].

The latter example reminds us of what Meinong pointed out in a somewhat different connection — "we can also count what does not exist."[26] For a man may be able to say truly "I fear exactly three people" where all three people are objects that do not exist.

Such intentional statements, then, are what provide the best possible case for Meinong's doctrine of *Außersein*. I think it must be conceded to Meinong that there is no way of paraphrasing any of them which is such that we know both (i) that it is adequate to the sentence it is intended to paraphrase and (ii) that it contains no terms ostensibly referring to objects that do not exist. Doubtless many philosophers are prejudiced against Meinong's doctrine because of the fact that Russell's theory of descriptions, as well as the theory of quantification in the way in which it is interpreted in *Principia Mathematica,* is not adequate to the statements with which Meinong

25. Thus Meinong's theory of value is based upon this assumption; see *Zur Grundlegung der allgemeinen Werttheorie,* Part II *("Die Werterlebnisse").*

26. "The Theory of Objects," English translation, p. 79; *Gesammelte Abhandlungen,* Vol. II, p. 487.

is concerned. But this fact, Meinong could say, does not mean that the statements in question are suspect. It means only that such logic, as it is generally interpreted, is not adequate to intentional phenomena.

CORRECT AND INCORRECT EMOTION

> "What affirmation and negation are in thinking, pursuit and avoidance are in desire; so that since moral virtue is a state of character concerned with choice, and choice is deliberate desire, therefore both the reasoning must be true and the desire right, if the choice is to be good, and the latter must pursue just what the former asserts. Now this kind of intellect, and of truth is practical; of the intellect which is contemplative, not practical or productive, the good and the bad state are truth and falsity, respectively (for this is the work of everything intellectual); while of the part which is practical and intellectual the good state is truth in agreement with right desire". (Aristotle, *Ethics*, VI, 2.)

The Analogy Between Judgment and the Emotions

Brentano's theory of correct and incorrect emotion is based upon the analogy he believes to hold between what he calls the sphere of the intellect and the sphere of the emotions. What he has to say about this presumed analogy seems to me to be very important indeed. Even where his views are controversial, they are extraordinarily suggestive, not only for ethics, but also for the theory of preference and for philosophical psychology.

Brentano usually describes the analogy in question as one that holds between "judgment", on the one hand, and "love and hate", on the other. But he uses the terms "love" and "hate" very broadly to refer, not only to what we might call "pro-emotions" and "anti-emotions", but also to what Aristotle called "pursuit" and "avoidance". We may put the analogy, in somewhat over-simplified form, first by noting certain facts about judgments and then by noting the corresponding facts about "love and hate".

Brentano divides judgments into two exclusive classes — those that are affirmative and those that are negative. Affirmative judgments are those that affirm, acknowledge, or accept something. Negative judgments are those that deny or reject something. All judgments are also either correct or incorrect; or, as we usually say, they are either true or false. And finally, there is a very close connection between the correctness and incorrectness of judgments, on the one hand, and *existence* and *non-existence*, on the other. For to say of an object that it *exists*, Brentano suggests, is to say that it is *correct to accept* that object, and to say of an object that it *does not exist* is to say that it is *correct to reject* that object. The latter point may also be put by saying that an object exists if and only if it is worthy of being accepted or affirmed, and that an object does not exist if and only if it is worthy of being rejected or denied.[1]

And now Brentano thinks, we may say much the same thing, *mutatis mutandis*, about emotions — about "love and hate".

Emotions are either positive or negative; they are either pro-emotions or anti-emotions, love or hate. Love and hate may be correct and they may also be incorrect. There is a very close connection between the correctness and incorrectness of emotions, on the one hand, and *goodness* and *badness* on the other. For to say of an object that it is *good*, Brentano suggests, is to say that it is *correct to love* that object, and to say of an object that it is *bad* is to say that it is *correct to hate* that object. The latter point may also be put by saying that an object is good if and only if it is worthy of being loved, and an object is bad if and only if it is worthy of being hated.

But to put the analogy this way is to oversimplify Brentano's doctrine. And, so he concedes, there are fundamental points of disanalogy that hold between the intellectual and the emotive spheres.

The Concept of Correctness

One might ask whether *any* instance of love or hate could be said to be correct or incorrect. How could one *defend* the doctrine that there are correct emotions and incorrect emotions? Here is a fundamental point with respect to which the views of Brentano and his followers are to be distinguished from those that have been associated with the Vienna Circle and subsequent logical empiricism. To understand

1. For the details of this view, see Brentano's *Wahrheit und Evidenz* (Hamburg: Felix Meiner, 1958; first published in Leipzig in 1930), ed., Oskar Kraus. The English edition is *The True and the Evident* (London: Routledge & Kegan Paul, Ltd., 1966), ed., Roderick M. Chisholm.

Brentano's attitude toward this question about emotive phenomena, we should consider its analogue in application to intellectual phenomena. What if one were to ask whether there are any *judgments* or *beliefs* that could be said to be correct or incorrect, to be true or false? How could one defend the doctrine that some beliefs or judgments are true or correct and that others are false or incorrect?

It is not difficuelt to see that, if there is a procedure by means of which we can defend the doctrine that there are correct judgments and incorrect judgments, then there will be an analogous procedure by means of which we can defend the doctrine that there are correct emotions and incorrect emotions.[2]

Brentano's procedure, in the case of intellectual phenomena, is to appeal to those judgments and beliefs that we *see*, directly and immediately, to be correct; or, as he puts it, those judgments and beliefs that are experienced as — or manifest themselves as being — correct (those judgments and beliefs that are "*als richtig charakterisiert*"). Such judgments may also be said to have a certain "inner correctness". These include judgements of "inner perception"; for example, the judgment that I am now thinking of a certain thing, the judgment that I seem to see such-and-such, and the judgment that I seem to remember so-and-so. The judgment that I now seem to see a cat, Brentano would say, is one that manifests itself as being correct. But it is the judgment that I *seem* to see a cat, or, as one might also put it, the judgment that I *think* I see a cat or *take* there to be a cat, and not the judgment that I *do* in fact see a cat, that thus manifests itself as being correct. And there are also certain "truths of reason" — for example, that there are no round squares — which are also experienced as being correct.[3]

It is in virtue of such directly evident facts as these, according to Brentano, that one first acquires the concept of correctness. The way in which we thus come to understand what it is for a belief or judgment to be correct is like the way in which we come to understand any other empirical concept. First we are presented with something that manifests that concept. Then, from such presenta-

2. It is significant to note that, in his lecture "On the Concept of Truth" (1889), Brentano appeals to the concept of the correctness of *emotion* in order to illuminate the concept of the correctness of judgment, rather than conversely. See *Wahrheit und Evidenz*, p. 25; *The True and the Evident*, p. 21.

3. See *Wahrheit und Evidenz*, p. 148ff.; *The True and the Evident*, p. 130ff.

tions of what is correct, we derive the concept of correctness. And, finally, given the concept of correctness, we are able to derive, by what is sometimes called "intuitive induction", certain general principles about correctness; for example, that no judgment that is correct contradicts any judgment that is correct. Such principles are all "apodictic" and "*a priori*". "But when we say that a certain type of knowledge is *a priori*, we do *not* mean to imply that the concepts which it involves can be given without perception and apperception".[4]

The correctness and incorrectness of emotion, Brentano says, are similar in these respects to the correctness and incorrectness of judgment. In *The Origin of Our Knowledge of Right and Wrong*, Brentano cites the following examples of emotions that "manifest themselves as being correct". First of all, the love of pleasure that we take in *insight* is a love or pleasure that we experience as being correct. So, too, the love that we have for joy — unless, Brentano significantly adds, "it be joy in what is bad". *Correct emotion* itself provides another example. Love of love that is correct is itself love that is correct. And, finally, every *thought or idea* is something that is good in itself, and "with every enrichment within the sphere of our ideas, regardless of the good or bad results that may happen to follow, the good within us is increased".[5] Love for this type of

4. Franz Brentano, *The Origin of Our Knowledge of Right and Wrong* (London: Routledge & Kegan Paul, 1969), translated by Roderick M. Chisholm and Elizabeth Schneewind; p. 113; *Vom Ursprung sittlicher Erkenntnis* (Third Edition, Leipzig: Feix Meiner, 1934), ed. Oskar Kraus; p. 111. The first edition of this work (Leipzig: Duncker und Humblot, 1889) was translated into English by Cecil Hague and published as *The Origin of our Knowledge of Right and Wrong* (London: Constable, 1902). Subsequent German editions of Brentano's book contain much important material, including the selection from which the above quotation is taken, which was not included in the first English edition. This new material is included in the 1969 edition; references in the present book to the English edition are to the 1969 edition.

5. *Vom Ursprung sittlicher Erkenntnis*, Third Edition, p. 23; *The Origin of our Knowledge of Right and Wrong*, p. 23. The final example — the value of enriching the sphere of our ideas — is developed in considerable detail in Brentano's writings on aesthetics. See Franz Brentano, *Grundzüge der Ästhetik* (Bern: Francke Verlag, 1959), ed. F. Mayer-Hillebrand, pp. 142-169.

intellectual enrichment also manifests itself as being correct.

Brentano spoke, then, of the "inner correctness" of certain judgments and emotions. It should be noted that he does *not* speak of the "inner *incorrectness*" of any judgment or emotion.

Correctness is not a Kind of Adequacy or Correspondence

Perhaps the best statement of Brentano's views about the nature of correctness is one that he sets forth in a letter written to Oskar Kraus, on March 21st, 1916. Brentano writes:

"What does it mean to say of a judgment or of an emotive attitude [*Gemütsbeziehung*] that it is correct? You say that this question has not been answered. And, according to you, we cannot see that such correctness obtains unless we have knowledge of an *adaequatio rei et intellectus* and of an *adaequatio rei et amoris*. But to me nothing could be easier than to show that this last is false. If it is necessary to have knowledge of an *adaequatio rei et intellectus*, then we find ourselves in an absurd *regressus in infinitum*. For how is one to know that there is a correspondence between the intellect and reality without first having knowledge both of the intellect and of reality? The correct answer, as I stated long ago, is this. The concept of correctness is made manifest to us in precisely the way in which other concepts are made manifest to us. We consider a multiplicity of things each of which exemplifies the concept and we direct our attention upon what these things have in common. Whenever I perceive that I judge with evidence I am aware of myself as someone who is judging correctly. The evidence of my own judgment also enables me to speak of the correctness of the judgments of other people: if anyone, however arbitrarily, arrives at an opinion which coincides with that of my own evident judgment then his opinion is correct, and if anyone arrives at an opinion that contradicts it then *his* opinion is not correct. And now, so far as the correctness of our emotive attitudes is concerned, we find that the situation is completely analogous. We know with immediate evidence that certain of our emotive attitudes are correct. And so we are able to compare the objects of these various attitudes and thus to arrive at the general concept of a correct emotion. Here, too, we will find that there are others whose emotive attitudes correspond with our own. If their attitudes should happen to be only a matter of habit or instinct, we may still say that they are correct but not that they are experienced as being correct [*als richtig charakterisiert*]. I cannot see any ground at all for reservations or misgivings about this. One can never find the criterion of correctness in an *adaequatio rei et intellectus vel amoris*; it can be found only in those attitudes which we know with immediate evidence to *be* correct".[6]

Emotive Phenomena are not Judgments

It is important to be clear that the emotive phenomena which are "characterized as being correct" are not *judgments of value.* Brentano observes, in the *Psychology*, that judgments of value presuppose presentations of good and bad; but such presentations, he says, can be derived only from the inner perception of emotions that are characterized as being correct. We derive the ideas of good and bad in precisely the same way we derive the ideas of truth and falsity. Brentano writes:

> If we say that every affirmative judgment is an act of taking something to be true, and every negative judgment an act of taking something to be false, this does not mean that the former consists in predicating truth of what is taken to be true and the latter in predicating falsity of what is taken to be false... What the expressions denote is a particular kind of intentional reception [*Aufnahme*] of an object, a distinctive kind of reference to a content of consciousness. The only correct interpretation is that anyone who takes something to be true will not only affirm the object, but, when asked whether the object is to be affirmed, will also affirm the object's to-be-affirmedness [*Anzuerkennensein*], i.e., its truth (which is all that is meant by this barbarous expression).[7]

Goodness and badness, Brentano then goes on to say, are *analogous* to truth and falsity. The words "good" and "bad", when used in connection with emotions that are characterized as being correct, signify "a distinctive way in which the mental act refers to a content".[8] Brentano then concludes: "A phenomenon belonging to this class is not a judgment. ('This is something to be loved', or 'This is something to be hated', would be judgments about goodness or

6. The letter is published in full in Franz Brentano, *Die Abkehr vom Nichtrealen* (Bern: Francke Verlag, 1966), ed. F. Mayer-Hillebrand, pp. 291-294; the passage here translated is on pp. 293-294. Compare also pp. 207-208, 305-306. The letter was also published in part in Oskar Kraus, *Franz Brentano: Zur Kenntnis seines Lebens und seiner Lehre* (Munich: Oscar Beck, 1919), pp. 31-33.

7. *Psychology*, p. 240; *Psychologie* II, 89.

8. *Psychology*, p. 240; *Psychologie* II, p. 90.

badness). It is, rather, an act of love or hate".[9]

These passages, from the first edition of the *Psychology*, show that Brentano was well on the way toward rejecting the usual concept of *adaequatio* or correspondence. For he had earlier maintained that the truth of an affirmative judgment consists in its correspondence with the *being* of its object and that the truth of a negative judgment consists in its correspondence with the *non-being* of its object. And he had also maintained earlier that the correctness of an emotion consists in its being in harmony (*im Einklange*) with the value of its object.[10]

The esential moments, then, of our knowledge of good and evil would seem to be the following.[11]

1. If we are to experience the inner correctness of an emotion, we must have an idea *Vorstellung* of this emotion. This means that the emotion must be one that we have experienced.

2. Once we have the idea of a given emotion, then we can contemplate that emotion without thereby feeling the emotion. Certain emotions are such that, in the course of this contemplation, they present themselves as being correct.

The emotion that is thus experienced as being correct may be either positive or negative. We could experience the inner correctness of the love of knowledge or of the hatred of sensuous pain. We can also experience the inner correctness of certain acts of preference.

The experience of the inner correctness of an emotion is analogous to the experience of the *evident*. For the inner correctness of certain judgments is what constitutes the evident. The difference is only that in the one case we are concerned with the inner correctness of a *judgment* and in the other case with the inner correctness of an *emotion*.[12]

The inner correctness of an emotion is not itself a feeling. That is to say, it is not a higher order emotion which has, the given emotion as its object.

9. *Ibid.*

10. See Kraus, *Die Werttheorien*, p. 217.

11. Compare Kraus, *Die Werttheorien*, p. 172.

12. Brentano often cites the evident judger as being an accident of the judger. It is interesting to note that he seldom cites "the person who experiences an emotion as being correct" as an accidnt of "the person who experiences an emotion".

3. The inner correctness of an emotion provides us with what is essential for making an apodictic value judgment — a judgment that is *a priori* and therefore *evident*. Being *a priori* the judgment "arises out of concepts" and is negative.

There is no difference in principle between apodictic value judgments and other apodictic judgments. Hence what Brentano says about the content of apodictic judgments generally also holds of such value judgments.

Some Disanalogies between Judgment and Emotion

According to Brentano's view, when we contemplate those *judgments* which are "experienced as being correct", we are able to abstract certain general "apodictic" principles about correctness. These principles form the basis of what is traditionally called logic and what also might be called "the theory of correct judgment". The same thing holds, he believes, for correct emotion and accordingly there is also "the theory of correct emotion."

Omitting certain details that are involved in Brentano's theory of judgment, we may formulate some of what he takes to be the basic principles of the theory of correct judgment in the following way:

1. It is impossible for there to be anything which is such that it may be correctly affirmed and also correctly denied.
2. It is impossible for there to be anything which is such that it may be incorrectly affirmed and also incorrectly denied.
3. It is impossible for there to be anything which is such that it may be correctly affirmed and also incorrectly affirmed.
4. It is impossible for there to be anything which is such that it may be correctly denied and also incorrectly denied.
5. It is impossible for there to be anything which is such that it may be neither incorrectly affirmed nor correctly denied.
6. It is impossible for there to be anything which is such that it may be neither incorrectly affirmed nor incorrectly denied.
7. It is impossible for there to be anything which is such that it may be neither correctly affirmed nor incorrectly affirmed.
8. It is impossible for there to be anything which is such that it may be neither correctly denied nor incorrectly denied.

These principles are objective and universal. Thus we may construe the first as telling us that, for *any* persons S and S', it is impossible for there to be anything which is such that it may be correctly affirmed by S and correctly denied by S'. S and S' may be the same person, in which case the principle tells us that it is impossible for there to be anything which is such that there is anyone who may correctly affirm and also correctly deny it. Or S and S' may be different persons, in which case the principle tells us that it is impossible for there to be anything which is such that there is one person who may correctly affirm it and another person who may correctly deny it. And analogously for the other principles. Brentano has sometimes been accused of what Frege and Husserl called "psychologism"; but the fact that he recognizes the universality and objectivity of such principles as the above indicates that the charge is unjustified.[13]

Following one traditional usage, we may say that principles (1) through (2) constitute the ground of *the law of contradiction* and that principles (5) through (8) constitute the ground of *the law of excluded middle.* Brentano's terminology is not orthodox, unfortunately, and he cites a version of (2) as being "the law of excluded middle".[14]

There is no doubt, according to Brentano, that the first four of these laws, those that we are calling the basis of the law of contradiction, have their analogues in the sphere of the emotions. Hence we may say that it is impossible for there to be anything which is such that it may be correctly loved and also correctly hated, or such that it may be incorrectly loved and also incorrectly hated, or such that it may be correctly loved and also incorrectly loved, or such that it may be correctly hated and also incorrectly hated. Brentano refers to the first of these principles as the "law of antagonism" and to the second, i.e., the principle according to which it is impossible for there to be anything which is such that it may be incorrectly loved and also incorrectly hated, as "the law of excluded middle for the sphere of the emotions".[15] And here, too, "psychologism" is false. For any subjects S and S', it is impossible for S to love correctly what S' hates

13. On Brentano and the charge of "psychologism", see Brentano's letter to Husserl in *Wahrheit und Evidenz*, pp. 152-159, and compare also pp. 63-64 and pp. 124-125 (*The True and the Evident*, pp. 135-138, 54-55, 110-111), as well as Oskar Kraus's introduction into the same work.

14. See Franz Brentano, *Die Lehre vom richtigen Urteil* (Bern: Francke Verlag, 1956), ed. F. Mayer-Hillebrand, p. 175.

15. See *Die Lehre vom richtigen Urteil*, p. 175: In the manuscript from which this section of *Die Lehre vom richtigen Urteil* was taken, Brentano cites a number of alternative labels for the emotive version of the first

correctly; and similarly for the other versions of the first four principles.

But what of the emotive analogues of the second four principles, i.e., (5) through (8), those principles which (unlike Brentano) we are associating with "the law of excluded middle"?

In *Vom Ursprung sittlicher Erkenntnis*, Brentano had said: "Of the two opposing attitudes, love and hate, being pleased and being displeased, in every instance one of them is correct and the other incorrect".[16] But Brentano was subsequently to revise his opinion".[17] And according to his later view, principles (5) through (8) do not hold for the sphere of the emotions.

Did Brentano accept a version of the "law of excluded middle" in application to the emotion? It is natural to take this question to mean: Did Brentano accept versions of principles (5) through (8) for the sphere of emotions? The answer to this question would be: *no*. But Brentano says, however, that he *does* accept of the principle of the "law of excluded middle" in application to the emotions. But in saying this, what he means is that a version of (2) applies to the emotions. In other words, he means that it is impossible for there to be anything which is such that it may be correctly loved and also incorrectly loved.

Hence the *indifferent* — that which is neither good nor bad — provides one important point of disanalogy between the sphere of judgment and the sphere of the emotions. Brentano seldom discusses the indifferent, but it is not difficult to see how this category would fit into his schema.[18] If the good in itself is that which it is correct to hate

principle; viz., "Gesetz des Antagonismus (des Widerstreits), Widerstrebens, Gegenfühlens, des Gegenstimmens, Gegengefühls, des Abneigens". The manuscript, listed as EL 4 in Brentano's *Nachlaß*, is entitled "Zur Axiomatik", and dated February 16, 1916.

16. Third edition, p. 19; *The Origin of our Knowledge of Right and Wrong*, p. 17-18.

17. Anton Marty, in the biographical sketch of Brentano he had prepared for the Engish edition of the *Ursprung*, i.e., *The Origin of our Knowledge of Right and Wrong*, called attention to this change in Brentano's views, p. 121-122. Unfortunately there is no indication in the book that this essay *was* written by Marty. The German version appears in Volume I of Marty's *Gesammelte Schriften* (Halle, 1916), p. 97ff.

18. See Oskar Kraus, *Die Werttheorien: Geschichte und Kritik* (Brunn: Verlag Rudolf M. Rohrer, 1937). In expounding Brentano's views, Kraus

and incorrect to love, then the *indifferent* in itself is that which it is neither correct nor incorrect to love and neither correct nor incorrect to hate. We should remind ourselves, therefore, that "not correct", in the sphere of the emotions, does not imply "incorrect", and that "not incorrect" does not imply "correct".

We have been discussing *intrinsic* goodness and badness — what is "good in itself" and "bad in itself". A thing is good (or bad) in itself, according to Brentano, if it is good (or bad) "regardless of the good or bad results that may happen to follow".[19] Brentano noted, however, that the terms "good" and "bad" are not always used to mean the same as "good in itself" and "bad in itself". They are also used more broadly to mean, respectively, "either good in itself or good as a means [*nützlich*]" and "either bad in itself or bad as a means [*schädlich*]". Taking the terms in this broader sense, he said, we may affirm that everything is either good or bad: i.e., everything is either such that it is good as an end or good as a means, or such that it is bad as an end or bad as a means. Otherwise, he said, there would be some things that God would have had no sufficient reason for creating.[20] "Love" and "hate" may also be used in this broader sense to mean respectively "love something either for its own sake, as an end, or as a means to something further that is loved for its own sake" and "hate something either for its own sake, as an end, or as a means to something further that is hated for its own sake." And if we take "love" and "hate" in this broader sense then we may affirm emotive analogues of principles (5) through (8) and hence an emotive analogue of the law of the excluded middle.

There is a further respect in which the sphere of the emotions may seem to differ from that of judgment. A compound or conjunction of the true and the false is false, no matter how much the true that is in it may outweigh the false. But a compound or whole that is made up of goods and evils may be good, provided that the good outweighs or otherwise makes up for the presence of evil. Is this a significant disanalogy between judgment and the emotions? We *could* after all,

writes: "The law of excluded middle has no analogue in the sphere of value; for there is that which is indifferent [es gibt Indifferentes]". (p. 174) The indifferent, he says, is that "in relation to which neither positive nor negative evaluation is justified; an example is that which is physical" pp. 196-7.

19. *Origin*, p. 23; *Ursprung*, p. 23. Compare *Origin*, p. 18; Ursprung, p. 19.

20. *Die Lehre vom richtigen Urteil*, p. 176.

say that a true conjunction is "more true" than its conjuncts, or that a conjunction with some true conjuncts is "more true" than a conjunction with no true conjuncts. The expression "more true" would then be analysable in terms of "contains more truths." The question becomes, then: is "better" analysable in terms of "contains more goods"? And the answer would seem to be no. Displeasure in the bad is better than pleasure in the bad — but it does not contain more goods, or fewer evils, than pleasure in the bad.[21]

21. If one holds that a heap of stones "has more being" than any one of the stones, then, presumably, what one says is to be analysed into "contains more *things*". Brentano observes, in another connection, that a cubic foot could be said to be "farther away from nothing [weiter vom Nichts ab]" than a cubic inch. This means, he says, that the former constitutes more *entia Realia* (mehr Reales) than does the latter. See *Untersuchungen zur Sinnespsychologie*, Second Edition (Hamburg: Felix Meiner Verlag, 1979), 193, 196-7.

OBJECTIVES AND INTRINSIC VALUE

1. Meinong made lasting contributions to almost every branch of philosophy. Among the most substantial of these are his writings on the theory of value, beginning with the *Psychologisch-ethische Untersuchungen zur Werttheorie*, in 1894, and ending with the posthumous *Zur Grundlegung der allgemeinen Werttheorie*, published in 1923, and the *Ethische Bausteine*, not published until 1968. Now, happily, Volume III of the *Meinong Gesamtausgabe* has appeared — *Abhandlungen zur Werttheorie*, published in Graz by the *Akademische Druck- u. Verlagsanstalt* in 1968, and edited by the late Hofrat Dr. Rudolf Kindinger. (I regret very much that the Hofrat cannot be with us. All friends of Meinong and of Austrian philosophy are deeply indebted to him). The *Abhandlungen zur Werttheorie* contain not only all of Meinong's published writings on the theory of value, but also the previously unpublished *Ethische Bausteine*, as well as extensive notes, addenda, and corrigenda that Meinong himself had made.

I will not attempt to summarize Meinong's contributions to the field. If one wants a general view of Meinong's place in the history of the theory of value, I would recommend these three writings: J.M. Findlay's *Meinong's Theory of Objects and Values*, published by Oxford in 1963; Karl Wolf's "*Die Grazer Schule: Gegenstandstheorie und Wertlehre*" published in *Philosophie in Österreich*, edited by Leo Gabriel and Johann Mader (Vienna: *Österreichischer Bundesverlag für Unterricht, Wissenschaft und Kunst*, 1968); and Oskar Kraus's somewhat less sympathetic account in *Die Werttheorien: Geschichte und Kritik* (Brünn: Rudolf M. Rohrer, 1937).[1] What I will do — I hope in the spirit of Meinong, or better, in the spirit of Brentano, Meinong and Mally — is discuss some of the consequences that

1. See also Wolf's "Die Entwicklung der Wertphilosophie in der Schule Meinongs", in *Meinong-Gedenkschrift* (Graz: "Styria" Steirische Verlagsanstalt, 1952), ed., K. Radakovic, A. Silva-Tarouca, and F. Weinhandl, pp. 157-171; and Kraus's "Die Grundlagen der Werttheorie", in *Philosophische Jahrbücher*, II. Jg. (1914), pp. 1-48.

follow if one makes certain general assumptions that Meinong had made in his later statements of his theory. I would say that the general assumptions are true but that some of their consequences are rather different from what Meinong took them to be.

The general assumptions are these. (1) There is — in Ernst Mally's terms — a logic of the emotions, or of the will, which can be formulated with precision.[2] (2) It is only after formulating this logic that one can deal adequately with the philosophical problems that cluster around the concept of value. (3) The primary sense of the term "value" pertains to intrinsic value — to what Meinong called "impersonal value [*unpersönlicher Wert*]"; this sense of the term is presupposed by the concepts of utility and instrumental value.[3] And (4) the bearers of intrinsic value — the objects to which value, in the primary sense of the term, may be ascribed — are all propositional objects. They are those objects, designatable by that-clauses, that were called *"Objektive"* by Meinong, *"Sachverhalte"* or "states of affairs" by Mally, and "propositions" by Russell.[4]

2. What are the things that are of intrinsic value? Meinong speaks of "logical", "aesthetic", and "timological" value.[5] He has in mind the value of knowledge and insight, the value of beauty and fittingness, and, as I interpret him, the value that is to be found in pleasure and in the exercise of virtue. The contraries of these things are the things that are intrinsically evil: error and ignorance, ugliness and unfittingness, displeasure and pain and the exercise of vice. Here Meinong carries on the tradition of Brentano.

It is obvious that the terms we have just used — "knowledge", "beauty", "fittingness", "pleasure", "exercise of virtue", "error", "ignorance", "ugliness", "displeasure", "pain", "exercise of vice" — do not designate *concreta*. In saying, for example, that *knowledge* is intrinsically good we mean, more exactly, that that state of affairs which is someone knowing something is intrinsically good. And in saying that pain is intrinsically bad, we mean that that state of affairs

2. See Ernst Mally, *Grundgesetze des Sollens: Elemente der Logik des Willens* (Graz: Leuschner & Lubensky, 1926), esp. pp. 1-8.

3. See *Abhandlungen zur Werttheorie*, pp. 280-282, 349, 404, 425 ff., 503, 625 ff.

4. See Chapter III ("Das Objektiv") of Meinong's *Über Annahmen*, Second Edition, (Leipzig: Johann Ambrosius Barth, 1910), and Mally, loc. cit.

which is someone being in pain ("someone experiencing painfully") is one that is intrinsically bad.

What is meant by saying of a state of affairs that it is *intrinsically* good — or *intrinsically* bad?

We may begin by noting this feature of intrinsic value. The intrinsic value of a state of affairs is the value that that state of affairs has *necessarily*. If a state of affairs is intrinsically good, it is intrinsically good in every possible world in which it obtains. And if it is intrinsically bad, it is intrinsically bad in every possible world in which it obtains. Thus what is *instrumentally* good, or good as a means, is a state of affairs that happens to lead to good results in this world, but it need not lead to good results in every possible world in which it obtains. And analogously for instrumental badness.

Following Brentano and Meinong we may also characterize the intrinsic value of a state of affairs by reference to the emotions which are *appropriate to* - or *required by* — that state of affairs. Let us illustrate this approach by reference to Meinong's theory of value.

Meinong held the following doctrine about the relation of value feelings (*Wertgefühle*) to intrinsic value. A state of affairs is intrinsically good if and only if *Seinsfreude* and *Nichtseinsleid* are the feelings that would be appropriate to it; and a state of affairs is intrinsically bad if and only if *Seinsleid* and *Nichtseinsfreude* are the feelings that would be appropriate to it.[5] In other words, a state of affairs is intrinsically good, if and only if, joy is the feeling that would be appropriate to its obtaining and sorrow is the feeling that would be appropriate to its not obtaining. And a state of affairs is intrinsically bad, if and only if, sorrow is the feeling that would be appropriate to its obtaining and joy is the feeling that would be appropriate to its not obtaining.

When Meinong thus says that a certain emotion is the emotion that is appropriate to — or required by — a given state of affairs, we should take him to mean that the emotion is one that is appropriate to the state of affairs *as such*. For the emotion that is appropriate to a given state of affairs *as such* may be quite different from the emotion

5. See *Abhandlungen zur Werttheorie*, p. 639; also page 124 of Meinong's "Selbstdarstellung", in Raymund Schmidt, ed., *Die Deutsche Philosophie der Gegenwart in Selbstdarstellungen*, Vol. I (Leipzig: Felix Meiner, 1921), pp. 91-150.

6. See *Abhandlungen zur Werttheorie*, pp. 410 ff., 562 ff., 640.

that is appropriate to any wider whole that that state of affairs might be thought to bring with it. The doctrine thus presupposes that, in the sphere of the emotions, there is a distinction that is analogous to the traditional distinction between the antecedent will and the consequent will: an antecedent emotion toward a state of affairs p is an emotion that is directed upon p as such; a consequent emotion toward a state of affairs p is an emotion that is directed upon a wider state of affairs that p is thought to bring with it.

I believe that Meinong's general approach to intrinsic value is correct. But we must modify what he says in one essential respect.

Meinong's doctrine, as we have set it forth, has the following consequence: a state of affairs is intrinsically good if and only if its negation is intrinsically bad. And this consequence seems to me to be false.

Let us first see why the consequence follows. Let p be a state of affairs that is intrinsically good — say, Mr. Smith knowing something. Joy, then, will be the emotion that is appropriate to p's being actual and sorrow will be the emotion that is appropriate to p's not being actual. But, as Meinong himself emphasizes, p's being actual is equivalent to not-p's not being actual, and p's not being actual is equivalent to not-p's being actual. Or, more barbarically, the actuality of p is equivalent to the nonactuality of not-p, and the nonactuality of p is equivalent to the actuality of not-p.[7] Hence if sorrow is appropriate to the nonactuality of p, then sorrow is also appropriate to the actuality of not-p. But, according to Meinong's doctrine, if sorrow is appropriate to the actuality of a state of affairs, then that state of affairs is intrinsically bad. Hence the actuality of not-p is intrinsically bad. But the actuality of not-p is equivalent to not-p. And therefore, according to Meinong's doctrine, if a state of affairs is intrinscially good then its negation is intrinsically bad. And analogously: if a state of affairs is intrinsically bad, then its negation is intrinsically good.

If this doctrine were true, then every possible world would contain an infinite amount of good and also an infinite amount of evil.[8] Consider this world, for example. There are no men who are ten feet tall. Hence our world contains such goods as these: no ten-foot man

7. See Meinong's discussion of the "Koinzidenz der Untatsächlichkeit mit der Tatsächlichkeit des Gegenteiles" in *Möglichkeit und Wahrscheinlichkeit* (Leipzig: Johann Ambrosius Barth, 1915), p. 94 ff.

8. Compare Kraus's criticism in *Die Werttheorien*, p. 227.

being in pain, no ten-foot man being in error, no ten-foot man behaving wickedly, and similarly for eleven-foot men, twelve-foot men, and so on *ad infinitum.* And our world contains such evils as these: no ten-foot man being in pleasure, no ten-foot man knowing anything, no ten-foot man behaving virtuously, and similarly for eleven-foot men, twelve-foot men, and so on *ad infinitum.* But, surely, in adding up the goods in this world it is not appropriate to list such facts as there being no ten-foot man in pain, and in adding up the evils is its not appropriate to list such facts as there being no ten-foot man who knows anything. A state of affairs is intrinsically good only to the extent that it entails the existence of pleasure, or knowledge, or beauty, or the exercise of virtue. But the nonexistence of a ten-foot man in pain does not entail any of these things and therefore it is not intrinsically good. And a state of affairs is intrinsically bad only to the extent that it entails the existence of displeasure, or error, or ugliness, or the exercise of vice. But the nonexistence of a ten-foot man who knows anything does not entail any of these things and therefore it is not intrinsically bad. Thus Aristotle said: "Positive goodness and badness are more important than the mere absence of goodness and badness: for positive goodness and badness are ends, which the mere absence of them cannot be".[9]

These facts have certain important consequences for the logic of the emotions. The negation of a good state of affairs will be neither good nor bad; and the negation of a bad state of affairs will be neither good nor bad. If by an *indifferent* state of affairs we mean a state of affairs having the same value as its negation, then the negations of good states of affairs and the negations of bad states of affairs will be themselves neither good, bad, nor indifferent. How, then are we to relate the fundamental concepts of the theory of value?

Instead of referring to four different emotions or feelings as Meinong does, let us make use of the concept of *preference* that had been emphasized by Brentano. One may be said to *prefer* one state of affairs to another. And one may be said to prefer one state of affairs *as such* to another. Let us say, then, that state of affairs p is *intrinsically preferable* to a state of affairs q, if and only if, for every x, the contemplation by x just of the conjunction of p and q requires that x prefer p to q as such.

9. *Rhetoric*, Book I, Ch. 7, 1364 a.

Now we are in a position to add the following definitions of our intrinsic value concepts. A state of affairs p is the *same in intrinsic value* as a state of affairs q, provided only p is not intrinsically preferable to q and q is not intrinsically preferable to p. A state of affairs is *intrinsically indifferent* provided only it is the same in value as its negation. A state of affairs is *intrinsically good* if and only if it is intrinsically preferable to a state of affairs that is intrinsically indifferent. A state of affairs is *intrinsically bad* if and only if a state of affairs that is intrinsically indifferent is intrinsically preferable to it. And a state of affairs is *intrinsically neutral* if and only if it is the same in value as a state of affairs that is indifferent.

For simplicity the qualification "intrinsically" will be left implicit in what follows.

One possibility is this. We take as our undefined concept that of one state of affairs being intrinsically preferable to another state of affairs. Then we set forth the following definitions. A state of affairs p is the *same in value* as a state of affairs q provided only p is not preferable to q and q is not preferable to p. A state of affairs is *indifferent* provided only it is the same in value as its negation. A state of affairs is *good* if it is preferable to a state of affairs that is indifferent, a state of affairs is *bad* if a state of affairs that is indifferent is preferable to it, and a state of affairs is *neutral* if it is the same in value as a state of affairs that is indifferent.

The following, I suggest, are plausible axioms: (A1) the relation of preferability is asymmetrical; (A2) the relation of not-being-preferable-to is transitive; (A3) all indifferent states of affairs are the same in value; (A4) all good states of affairs are preferable to their negation; (A5) all bad states of affairs have negations that are preferable to them; (A6) if a disjunction of two states of affairs is preferable to a given state of affairs, then either the one disjunct is preferable to the given state of affairs or the other disjunct is preferable to the given state of affairs; (A7) if a given state of affairs is preferable to a disjunction of two states of affairs, then the given state of affairs is preferable either to the one disjunct or to the other disjunct; (A8) every state of affairs that is entailed by the tautology, p or not-p, is indifferent; and finally, (A9) any two states of affairs that entail each other are the same in value.[10]

10. The definitions of the value concepts above and the first axioms are from Roderick M. Chisholm and Ernest Sosa, "On the Logic of 'Intrinsically Better' ", *American Philosophical Quarterly*, Vol. III (1966), pp. 244-249.

Among the consequences of these axioms are the following: sameness of intrinsic value is transitive, reflexive, and symmetrical; intrinsic preferability is transitive, irreflexive and asymmetrical; goodness, badness, and neutrality are exclusive and exhaustive; what is good is preferable to what is neutral; what is neutral is preferable to what is bad; whatever is preferable to what is good is itself good; whatever what is bad is preferable to is itself bad; nothing that is good has a negation that is good; and nothing that is bad has a negation that is bad.

The neutral turns out to be wider than the indifferent. For although all indifferent states of affairs are neutral and all neutral states of affairs are the same in value, there will be some neutral states of affairs that are not indifferent: these will be the negations of good states of affairs and the negations of bad states of affairs. And so where Meinong would say the negation of a good state of affairs is bad, or that the negation of a bad state of affairs is good, we say that it is neutral.

3. This way of looking at intrinsic value throws light upon what G.E. Moore called "the principle of organic unities" — a principle he expressed by saying "the value of... a whole bears no regular proportion to the sum of the values of its parts", and "the value of a whole must not be assumed to be the same as the sum of the values of its parts".[11] The principle is readily illustrated in terms of what Meinong, in the *Ethische Bausteine*, called "*Sekundärwerthaltungen*" — the ways in which one man may value the ways in which another man may share in value.[12]

We may suppose that joy is good and sorrow is bad. Consider now the joy or sorrow that one man may take in another man's joy or sorrow. There are these possibilities: *Mitfreude*, or joy in the other man's joy; *Mitleid*, or sorrow in the other man's sorrow; *Schadenfreude*, or joy in the other man's sorrow; and envy or *Neid* — sorrow in the other man's joy. Though Meinong is not clear about this point, let us take these terms intentionally so that the occurrence of these "*Sekundärwerthaltungen*" on the part of the one man will not imply the existence of the corresponding "*Primärwerthaltung*" on the part

11. G.E. Moore, *Principia Ethica* (Cambridge: The University Press, 1903), pp. 27, 28.

12. *Abhandlungen zur Werttheorie*, pp. 712-718.

of the other. Saying that a man experiences *Mitfreude*, then, will be to say that he experiences joy in what he takes to be the fact that another man experiences joy, but it will not imply that anyone actually does experience joy. And analogously for the other terms: I may envy you for what I take to be your good fortune without it being the case that you actually have ever *had* good fortune.

Given an ethics such as that of Brentano, *Schadenfreude* and *Mitleid* provide clear cases of what Moore called organic unities: they are wholes having a value that is not proportional to the sum of the values of their parts.[13] We have assumed that joy is good and that sorrow is bad. Suppose, then, we go on to say that that joy which is joy in another man's sorrows is neutral and therefore neither good nor bad, and that that sorrow which is sorrow in another man's sorrow is also neutral and therefore neither good nor bad. If, now, conforming to Moore's terminology, we call any state of affairs a "whole" and any state of affairs entailed by such a whole a "part" of that whole, we may say that *Schadenfreude* is a neutral whole that has a good part but no bad part. Taking pleasure in what one takes to be another man's sorrow has a good part — there being pleasure. It has no bad part — for, as we have seen, taking pleasure in what one takes to be another man's sorrow does not imply that there *is* such sorrow, and it does not imply the existence of any other evil. If the whole has a good part, and no bad parts and is nevertheless neutral, then surely is has a value that is not proportionate to the value of the sum of its parts. And analogously for *Mitleid*. If it has a bad part (there being sorrow), has no good parts, and is nevertheless neutral, then it, too, has a value that is not proportionate to the value of the sum of its parts.

Such "organic unities" are to be contrasted with what Moore called "mere sums" — wholes having a value that *is* proportionate to the sum of the values of their parts. An example would be that whole which is Jones taking pleasure in the being of stones and Smith taking displeasure in the being of stones. This whole has a good part and a bad part which balance each other off with the result that the

13. See the discussion of pleasure in the bad ("Lust am Schlechten") and displeasure in the bad ("Unlust am Schlechten") in Franz Brentano, *Ursprung sittlicher Erkenntnis*, Third Edition (Leipzig: Felix Meiner, 1934), pp. 84-86. This discussion may be found in the English edition, *The Origin of Our Knowledge of Right and Wrong* (London: Routledge & Kegan Paul, 1969), edited by Roderick M. Chisholm.

whole is itself neutral. But the good part of that whole which is *Schadenfreude* is not balanced off by any bad part; yet the result is neutral. And the bad part of that whole which is *Mitleid* is not balanced off by any good part; yet the result is neutral. One might say that in the case of *Schadenfreude* the goodness of one of the parts is *defeated* by the larger whole and that in the case of *Mitleid* the badness of one of the parts is *defeated* by the larger whole.[14]

These concepts, I believe, are captured by the following definitions. We will say that an *Objektiv* or state of affairs p is *part* of an *Objektiv* or state of affairs q, provided only p entails q. Following Moore, we will say that a *mixed whole* is one having good parts and bad parts and an *unmixed whole* is one that is not mixed. (Given our assumptions, every whole, whether good or bad and whether mixed or unmixed, will have neutral parts). Let us say that a state of affairs p *falls in value between* two states of affairs, q and r, provided that either (a) q is preferable to p and p is preferable to r or (b) r is preferable to p and p is preferable to q. We may now say that a state of affairs p is an *organic whole*, or an *organic unity*, provided only the following condition holds: either (a) p is a mixed whole and does not fall in value between any two of its parts or (b) p is unmixed and either has a good part that is better than p or has a bad part that is worse than p. Thus *Schadenfreude* is an organic unity, by this definition, since it is an unmixed whole (it has a good part but no bad part) and has a good part that is better than it; and *Mitleid* is an organic unity since it is an unmixed whole and has a bad part that is worse than it. On the other hand, that neutral state of affairs which is Jones taking pleasure in the being of stones and Smith taking displeasure in the bing of stones is not an organic unity, for it is a mixed whole that falls in value between two of its parts. A state of affairs which is thus not an organic unity might be said to be a *mere sum*.

If a whole is an organic unity then it could be said to *defeat* — wholly or partially — the value of some of its parts. Thus *Schadenfreude* is a neutral whole which wholly defeats the goodness of one of its parts and *Mitleid* is a neutral whole which wholly defeats the

14. For other examples and a more detailed discussion of defeat, see Roderick M. Chisholm, "The Defeat of Good and Evil", *Proceedings and Addresses of the American Philosophical Association*, Vol. XLII (1968-69), pp. 21-38.

badness of one of its parts. These concepts may be defined as follows.

The goodness of a state of affairs p is *wholly defeated* by wider state of affairs q provided that: p is part of q, p is good, q is not good, and any part of q that is worse than q is part of p. And the badness of a state of affairs p is wholly defeated by a wider state of affairs q provided that: p is part of q, p is bad, q is not bad, and any part of q that is better than q is part of p.

Total defeat, thus defined, may be contrasted with partial defeat. The goodness of a state of affairs p may be said to be *partially defeated* by a wider state of affairs q provided that: p is part of q, p is good, p is better than q, and any part of q that is bad is part of p. And the badness of a state of affairs p may be said to be partially defeated by a wider state of affairs q provided that: p is part of q, p is bad, q is better than p, and any part of q that is good is part of p. (What would illustrate partial defeat? Consider a man's being justly *punished* for a wicked deed, according to the retributivist view: it entails that evil which is the performance of the misdeed; it contains a further evil which is the suffering and disgrace of the man who is punished; but this suffering and disgrace — according to retributivism — makes things better than they would otherwise have been. And so on this view the whole situation — the punishment of the man who performed the wicked deed — may be bad but it is better than that part of it which is just the performance of the wicked deed. Hence the badness of that performance is partially defeated; for the whole, though bad, is better than *it* is, and the whole, having no good parts at all, has no good parts that are not part of the wicked performance.[15]

4. One further concept, suggested in Meinong's writings, may be of fundamental importance for the theory of value. The bearers of value according to Meinong, are *Objektive,* or *states of affairs*. Meinong also used the term *"Dignitive"* for objects of feeling (and "*Desiderativa*" for objects of desire).[16] What distinguishes a *Dignitativum* from

15. Thus Brentano held in an unpublished fragment that a bad state in combination with sorrow could be better than that same bad state in combination with pleasure, and cites vindictive punishment, repentance, and atonement as possible examples. The fragment, listed in Brentano's *Nachlass* as Ethik 1, is entitled "Vom Guten, das in der Zuordnung liegt".

16. See *Abhandlungen zur Werttheorie*, pp. 397, 401, 636, and Meinong's "Selbstdarstellung", p. 110.

an *Objektivum*? I am not certain that I have understood Meinong, but it may be that he has the following concept in mind.

Let us say that an *Objektivum* or state of affairs p is a *V-state* provided only that p is a nonneutral state of affairs which is such that, for every q, if p entails q and q has the same value as p, then q entails p. A V-state is thus a minimal value state. Jones being happy is not a V-state, for it entails someone being happy which has the same value as it but does not entail it. It being the case both that Jones is happy and Jones' wife is happy is not a V-state, for it entails two people being happy which has the same value as it but which does not entail it. But presumably these are V-states: someone being happy, someone acting virtuously, someone being unhappy, it being the case that the amount of unhappiness is greater than the amount of happiness.

It is possible that Meinong was thinking of V-states when he spoke of "*Dignitive*". Perhaps the following will indicate why I believe the concept to be of fundamental importance for the theory of value.

We may say "the value of a state of affairs is a function of the value of the V-states it entails" and explicate this as follows: (1) Every nonneutral state of affairs p entails a set of V-states such that the conjunction of them all has the same value as p. (2) A state of affairs p is preferable to a state of affairs q, if and only if: either (a) the conjunction of all the V-states that p entails is preferable to the conjunction of all the V-states that q entails; or (b) p entails no V-states and the conjunction of all the V-states that q entails is bad; or (c) q entails no V-states and the conjunction of all the V-states that p entails is good. And (3) a state of affairs p has the same value as a state of affairs q, if and only if: either (a) the conjunction of all the V-states that p entails has the same value as the conjunction of all the V-states that q entails; (b) one entails no V-states and the conjunction of all the V-states that the other entails is neutral; or (c) neither entails any V-states.

If we apprehend the value of a V-state, we do so directly. One way of apprehending the value of a state of affairs which is not a V-state is this: We first determine what V-states it entails. If we find that it entails no V-states, we know that it is neutral. If we find that it does entail V-states, we then attempt to apprehend the value of that V-state which is the conjunction of all the V-states it entails. Is there a general formula by means of which the value of a disjunction, pvq, can be exhibited as a function of the value of its disjuncts? There is this: "Consider the worst in p and the worst in q, and take whichever one r is not worse than the other; consider the best in p and the best in q, and take whichever one s is not better than the other. Then: (1) pvq has the same value as r&s; (2) if r is bad and s is neutral, then pvq has the same value as r; and (3) if s is good and r is neutral, then pvq has the same value as s". In applying this formula, we assume that every state of affairs implies some neutral state of affairs. Is there, analogously, a general formula by means of which the value of a conjunction can be exhibited as a function of the value of its conjuncts? It would seem not. For the conjunction may imply something about the distribution of value which is not implied by either conjunct separately; and the value of the conjunction may be a function of this distribution as well as of the amount of value in its conjuncts. Hence our only recourse is to determine what V-states the conjunction entails and then to try to apprehend directly the value of *their* conjunction.

There are many unanswered questions, then, in the theory of value and in the area of the logic of the emotions. I hope that those who work in the field will continue to follow in the footsteps of Brentano, Moore, and Meinong.

THE QUALITY OF PLEASURE AND OF DISPLEASURE

Introduction

Brentano's sensitivity to the facts of intentionality enables him to find a straightforward answer to the questions: In what sense may we speak of the *quality* of pleasure and displeasure? Pleasure and displeasure may take intentional objects. Just as one may *believe that* Smith is happy, or *know that* Smith is happy, one may also be *pleased that* Smith is happy, or be *displeased that* Smith is happy. In the case of those pleasures and displeasures, then, that thus have intentional objects, there is an obvious way of making qualitative distinctions: the quality of the pleasure or displeasure will be a function of the intrinsic value of the *intentional object* of the pleasure or displeasure. One pleasure is better than another pleasure if the intentional object of the one is better than the intentional object of the other; and one displeasure is *worse* than another displeasure if the intentional object of the one is *better* than the intentional object of the other.

Brentano does not put the matter in just that way that I have put it. But he considers and contrasts the four possibilities, "pleasure in the good," "pleasure in the bad," "displeasure in the good," and "displeasure in the bad." On the basis of what he says, one could formulate a general theory of the qualities of pleasure. Let us consider one possible theory, which seems to accord with Brentano's own.

Brentano's Approach

Brentano recognizes a category of that which is intrinsically indifferent or neutral — of that which is neither good in itself nor bad in itself. Hence we could begin with the following principle (though Brentano does not explicitly mention it):

(1) Pleasure in the neutral is good.

If a man is pleased, say, that there are flowers in the world, where there being flowers is something that is intrinsically indifferent, then his innocent pleasure is good. And analogously for displeasure:

(2) Displeasure in the neutral is bad.

We should note that, according to Brentano's theory of value, (2) differs from (1), in the following respect: whereas (1) implies the existence of a good and does *not* imply the existence of an evil, (2) implies the existence of an evil and *also* implies the existence of a good — namely the existence of consciousness, someone being aware of something. Brentano's view seems to be that all evil involves good whereas it is not the case that all good involves some evil. (Here, then, is a fundamental point at which the analogy between the sphere of judgment and the sphere of the emotions is incomplete: the existence of what is intrinsically evil always implies the existence of something that is intrinsically good, just as the false always implies something that is true; but whereas the existence of what is good may also imply the existence of what is evil, the true never implies anything that is false.[1])

Given principles (1) and (2) above, we may go on to say, as Brentano does:

(3) Pleasure in the good is good;
(4) Displeasure in the good is bad.

If you are pleased that Smith is pleased that there are flowers in the world, then your pleasure is good; and if I am displeased that Smith is pleased that there are flowers in the world, then my displeasure is bad.

We could now add the following four principles of intrinsic preferability:

(5) Pleasure in the good is preferable to pleasure in the neutral;
(6) Displeasure in the bad is preferable to displeasure in the neutral;
(7) Pleasure in the good is preferable to pleasure in the bad;
(8) Displeasure in the bad is preferable to displeasure in the good.

1. See *Religion und Philosophie*, Hamburg: Felix Meiner 1974, pp. 173-179, and *Grundlegung und Aufbau der Ethik*, Hamburg: Felix Meiner 1978, pp. 184, 192; *The Foundation and Construction of Ethics*, London: Routledge & Kegan Paul 1973, 169-170, 176-177. Another version of the relevant material in *Religion und Philosophie* is published as "Optimismus," in Samuel Hugo Bergmann, "Unbekannte Manuskripte Franz Brentanos", in *Horizons of a Philosopher: Essays in Honor of David Baumgardt*, ed. J. Frank, H. Minkowski, and E.J. Sternglass, Leiden: E.J. Brill 1963, pp. 34-49; "Optimismus" appears on pp. 35-39.

Brentano does not discuss principles (5) and (6), but he explicitly affirms (7) and (8).

Further principles relating the quality and *quantity* of pleasure and displeasure should now be obvious.

Two Difficult Cases

What are we to say of pleasure in the bad — my pleasure, say, that Smith is experiencing unjustified pain? Brentano says: "Pleasure in the bad, to the extent that it is pleasure, is something that is good, but to the extent that it is at the same time an incorrect emotion, it is something that is bad. It is not purely bad, but it is predominantly bad. In avoiding it as being something bad, we are not exercising a simple act of hate; rather we are exercising an act of preference. We prefer being free from what is bad in this situation to being in possession of what is good. Here we have an act of preference which is seen to be correct and which justifies our avoidance of pleasure in the bad. We say to ourselves: 'Better that there be no pleasure at all than pleasure in the bad.' "[2]

Should we say, perhaps, that pleasure in the bad is *both* good and bad, though predominantly bad? Not if what Brentano had called "the law of antagonism" is valid. For, according to this law, nothing is such that it may be both correctly loved and also correctly hated. And therefore, given Brentano's definitions of "good" and "bad," nothing is such that it is both good and bad.[3] Hence we must take a more positive stand toward pleasure in the bad and say of it either that it is good, or that it is bad, or that it is neutral. And there seems to be no doubt about Brentano's view. He would say:

(9) Pleasure in the bad is bad.

We may be tempted to say that pleasure in the bad is neutral and not bad. But this would not be in the spirit of Brentano's view. For pleasure in the bad, he says, *is* an incorrect emotion, and an incorrect emotion is something that is bad.[4] Pleasure in the bad, then, is what

2. *Grundlegung und Aufbau der Ethik,* p. 213; *The Foundation and Construction of Ethics,* p. 196. Compare *Vom Ursprung sittlicher Erkenntnis,* Hamburg: Felix Meiner 1978, p. 85; *The Origin of Our Knowledge of Right and Wrong,* London: Routledge & Kegan Paul 1970, p. 90-1.

3. Compare *Vom Ursprung sittlicher Erkenntnis,* p. 150; *The Origin of Our Knowledge of Right and Wrong,* p. 145.

4. See *Origin,* p. 90.

G. E. Moore called a "mixed evil"; it is bad, but it involves *some* good.

What about displeasure in the bad? This, Brentano says, is not *purely* good, but it is *predominantly* good.[5] It seems clear, then, that he would say:

(10) Displeasure in the bad is good.

Displeasure in the bad, therefore, is what Moore called a "mixed good"; it is good, but it involves some evil.

Principles (9) and (10) are also relevant to the question of the analogy between correctness in the sphere of the intellect and correctness in the sphere of the emotions. There are "mixed falsehoods," since, for example, there are false conjunctions with true conjuncts. But, although there are "mixed goods", there are no "mixed truths." The presence of one falsehood, however trivial, will turn a conjunction into a falsehood, however impressive the other conjuncts may be. But the addition of a trivial evil will not, *ipso facto*, turn a good situation into a bad one.

If we are justified in attributing principles (9) and (10) to Brentano, then we may also attribute to him the following:

(11) Displeasure in the bad is preferable to pleasure in the bad.

The Value of Emotive Indifference

Should we extend our principles to emotive indifference? One's attitude toward a given state of affairs may be said to be one of indifference provided one contemplates the state of affairs and is neither pleased nor displeased with it. To the extent that such indifference involves contemplation it is good — according to Brentano's principles. But to what extent is its value affected by the value of its intentional object?

According to a rigoristic ethics, indifference toward the good and indifference toward the bad would both be bad; only indifference toward the neutral would be such that it is not bad. It is true, of course, that one should not be indifferent toward the good or indifferent toward the bad. But does it follow from this that *every* instance of an indifferent contemplation of the good — or of an

5. Compare *Grundlegung und Aufbau,* p. 214; *Foundation and Construction,* pp. 196-7; *Vom Ursprung,* p. 85; *Origin,* p. 90-91.

indifferent contemplation of the bad — is intrinsically bad? It does not seem to me that it does. I would say, therefore, that such indifference is *not* intrinsically bad. And indeed, since it implies an active contemplation of a state of affairs, it is intrinsically good.

A Table of Values

There are three fundamental types of intrinsic value: the intrinsically good, the intrinsically bad, and the intrinsically neutral. And there are three emotive attitudes: pro-attitude, anti-attitude, and emotive indifference. Hence we may construct the following table, wherein the top line refers to the possible states of value and the first colum refers to the emotive attitudes.

	Good	Bad	Neutral
Pro-attitude			
Anti-attitude			
Indifference			

The first space — following "Pro-attitude" and under "Good" — would be used to indicate our evaluation ("good", "bad", or "neutral") of a pro-attitude that is directed upon a state of affairs that is intrinsically good. The second space — following "Pro-attitude" and under "Bad" — would be used to indicate our evaluation of a pro-attitude that is directed upon a state of affairs that is intrinsically bad. And analogously for the other places. We will use the letters "G", "B" and "N", respectively, to abbreviate "intrinsically good", "intrinsically bad", and "intrinsically neutral."

If what we have said is correct, our table of values should be completed as follows:

	Good	Bad	Neutral
Pro-attitude	G	B	G
Anti-attitude	B	G	B
Indifference	G	G	G

But given a more rigoristic ethics, the line for emotive indifference would filled in differently:

	Good	Bad	Neutral
Pro-attitude	G	B	G
Anti-attitude	B	G	B
Indifference	B	B	N

We should remind ourselves that "indifference" is here taken to refer to an active mental state: one is emotionally indifferent toward a given state of affairs provided only one contemplates that state of affairs and is neither pleased nor displeased with it. But we could take "indifferent" purely negatively: one would then be said to be indifferent toward a given state of affairs only if one is neither pleased nor displeased with that state of affairs. If we take "indifferent" in this negative way, then all three entries in the bottom line of our table should be replaced by "N."

SUPEREROGATION AND OFFENCE:

A Conceptual Scheme for Ethics

1. Is it always wrong not to do what is right? Or bad not to do what is good? Such questions arise when we consider the relation between what is our duty to do and what is sometimes called 'supererogation,' and the relation between what it is our duty not to do and what I shall here call 'offence.' There are reasons for answering both questions in the negative and I shall consider some of these reasons — not, however, to provide an answer to the two questions, but to throw light upon our moral concepts. I shall suggest that one familiar three-fold classification of moral concepts is inadequate; I shall then consider an alternative proposed by Meinong which has certain advantages but which, I believe, is also inadequate; and finally, I shall propose a cenceptual scheme of my own, with the hope that it may throw light, not only upon the relations among our moral concepts, but also upon different types of moral system.

2. There are some things, within our power either to do or not to do, which we *must* do or *have* to do, whatever we may desire. And there are other things, similarly within our power, which we must *not* do, no matter what we may happen to desire. Let us say that it is our *duty* to do things of the first sort and not to do things of the second sort. To have a convenient shorthand, we may say, perhaps contrary to ordinary usage, that actions of the first sort are *obligatory* and those of the second *forbidden*; we may also say, of the things that are within our power either to do or not to do, that whatever is not forbidden is *permitted*, and whatever is not obligatory is *non-obligatory*, or *unrequired*.[1]

If an act is one which, in the present sense, we *must* perform, then it

1. I say that the shorthand is probably contrary to ordinary usage for this reason: 'obligatory,' as ordinarily used, may suggest a prior contract or commitment, and 'forbidden' and 'permitted' may suggest a commander or lawgiver; but the expressions containing 'must' which these terms abbreviate need carry none of these suggestions.

is one which we *must not* refrain from performing; and if an act is one which we must not perform, then it is one which we must refrain from performing. Again, if an act is one which we *may* perform, then it is one which we *need not* refrain from performing; and if it is one which we need not perform then it is one which we may refrain from performing. It is now a commonplace that the logical relations among these concepts may be exhibited in the traditional square of opposition. For any act A, which it is within our power either to perform or not to perform, the square tells us: if A is obligatory then A is permitted, but not conversely; if A is forbidden then A is non-obligatory; and A is forbidden if and only if A is not permitted.[2] It follows that everything in our power is such that it is either obligatory, or forbidden, or both permitted and non-obligatory.

According to some recent authors, if an act is both permitted and non-obligatory, it may be said to be *morally indifferent.*[3] Hence, if these authors are right, it will follow from what we have just said that everything within our power is either obligatory, forbidden, or morally indifferent. But, according to others, certain things within our power are neither obligatory, nor forbidden, nor morally indifferent — i.e. certain acts are both permitted and non-obligatory and yet *not* morally indifferent. Examples are provided by those actions which are sometimes called 'supererogatory.'

I shall now state the case for saying that certain acts of supererogation are thus neither obligatory, forbidden, nor morally indifferent. Then I shall point out — what seems to have been overlooked in recent moral philosophy — that the class of supererogatory acts has a complement; acts of this second sort I shall call (for lack of a better term) 'offences.' We may say of offences, as well as of acts of supererogation, that they are neither obligatory,

2. The relationships were first pointed out, so far as I know, by Alois Höfler, in 'Abhängigkeitsbeziehungen zwischen Abhängigkeitsbeziehungen,' *Sitzungsberichte der kaiserlichen Akademie der Wissenschaften in Wien*, Bd. CLXXXI (1917), pp. 1-56. Höfler's terms were 'Geboten,' 'Verboten,' 'Erlaubt,' and 'Nicht geboten' (p.41). He noted that this part of his article was taken from a manuscript he had written in 1885.

3. Compare G.H. von Wright, 'Deontic Logic,' *Mind*, vol. LX (1951), pp. 1-13; *An Essay in Modal Logic*, Amsterdam 1951, chapter v; A.N. Prior, *Formal Logic,* Oxford 1955, pp. 221 ff.; Alan Ross Anderson, *The Formal Analysis of Normative Systems,* New Haven 1956.

forbidden nor morally indifferent.

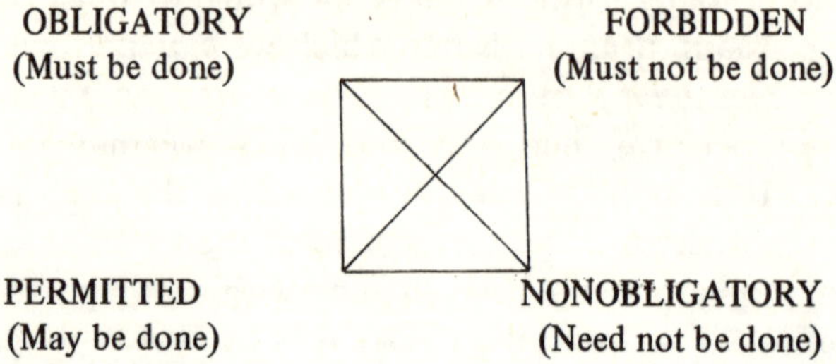

3. John Ladd, in *The Stucture of a Moral code*, and more recently J. O. Urmson, writing on 'Saints and Heroes,' pointed out that those acts which we are calling 'supererogatory' fall outside of the three-fold classification we have just described; Ladd said that these are 'acts which it is right to do, but not wrong not to do.'[4] Etymologically, the term 'supererogatory' suggests that which is 'over and above what is called for'; hence those acts which are 'over and above the call of duty' might properly be called 'supererogatory.'[5] But let us think of the supererogatory, more generally, as that which it is good, but not obligatory, to do. Some of the great deeds of saints and heroes were thus supererogatory: these deeds were not obligatory, they were not forbidden, and they were not morally indifferent since they were good things to do.

But if we take the supererogatory to be that which it is good but not obligatory to do, in short, if we take it to be 'non-obligatory well-doing,' then we must not identify it with saintliness or heroism. For, as Ladd points out, contributing small change to the Home for Little Wanderers may be supererogatory in this sense: it is good and therefore not indifferent; it is neither obligatory nor forbidden; and, in most cases, it is neither saintly nor heroic. The same may be said, perhaps, for being kind to animals, for ordinary politeness, and, as Feinberg notes, for most of those acts which we ordinarly call 'favours.'

4. John Ladd, *The Structure of a Moral Code*, Cambridge, Mass. 1957, p. 127; J.O. Urmson, 'Saints and Heroes,' in A. Melden, ed., *Essays in Moral Philosophy*, Seattle 1958. Compare also Joel Feinberg, 'Supererogation and Rules,' *Ethics*, vol. 71 (1961), pp. 276-88, and the reference to Meinong below.

5. Feinberg's paper, cited above, is a lucid discussion of 'duty plus,' as this concept has been understood in Western morals and theology.

In order to see what supererogation or 'non-obligatory well-doing,' is *not*, let us contrast these four acts:

(1) keeping one's promise to return a book;
(2) sacrificing one's life in the performance of duty;
(3) conferring a small favour by lending a book;
(4) sacrificing one's life in a non-obligatory rescue.

We can image the circumstances under which these acts are done to be such that, under those circumstances, the first two acts are duties and the last two supererogatory. We can imagine further that these circumstances are, in addition, such that the first and third acts are trifling and the second and fourth heroic and magnificent. And we can imagine, finally, that what is accomplished by the two heroic acts is considerably better than what is accomplished by the two acts which are trifling. If all of this is so, then we may draw certain negative conclusions.

The difference between supererogation and duty, or moral obligation, cannot be decribed by saying that acts of supererogation are necessarily *more praiseworthy*, or of *greater merit*, or *better* in their overall consequences, than are acts of duty. For if we contrast the man who performs an heroic act of duty with the man who performs a trifling act of supererogation, that is, if we contrast the man of (2) with the man of (3), we can say that the obligatory act of the former is better, of greater merit, and more deserving of praise than is the supererogatory act of the latter.

Nor can the difference between supererogation and duty be described by saying that supererogation, unlike duty, implies certain virtues in the agent. The man who performs an act of supererogation does, of course, have the virtue of being such that he is led to perform it, but beyond this, so far as the concept of supererogation is concerned, he may share his traits of character with the man who confines his good deeds to those things it is his duty to do.

Nor, finally, can the difference between duty and supererogation be made out by reference to the traditional distinction between those duties which are 'perfect' and those which are 'imperfect.' The latter distinction was drawn by Mill as follows: 'Duties of perfect obligation are those duties in virtue of which a correlative *right* resides in some person or persons; duties of imperfect obligation are those which do not give birth to any right.'[6] If I have more than my share of

6. *Utilitarianism*, chapter v. The distinction has also been put more

the goods of the world and am obliged to surrender my surplus to you, and only to you, then you have a right which is correlative with my obligation, and the obligation, therefore, is a 'perfect' one. But if I am obligated to surrender my goods only to *someone or other*, whom I may select myself, then there is no one having a right correlative with my obligation, and the obligation, therefore, is 'imperfect.' Let us suppose that I have such an 'imperfect' obligation and pick Mr. Jones as the one who is to receive my goods. Since I was not obligated to pick *him* it may be tempting to infer that, when I do present my goods to him, I have performed an act of 'non-obligatory well-doing' and hence, according to our description, an act of supererogation. But this inference would be a mistake. My 'imperfect' obligation was that of giving to Jones *or* to Robinson. . . *or* to Smith; in giving to Jones, I do, *ipso facto*, give to Jones *or* to Robinson . . . *or* to Smith; hence I do fulfil my entire obligation, and it would be incorrect, therefore, to suppose that the act is a case of 'non-obligatory well-doing' and hence supererogatory.

The status of supererogation might be summarized in this way. If I seek advice, concerning an act which would be supererogatory, and ask 'Shall I do this?", I may well be told, 'You *ought* to, but you don't *have* to' — it is advisable, but not obligatory.

Is it ever appropriate to say, similarly, 'You ought *not* to, but you *may*?'

4. A system of moral concepts which provides a place for what is good but not obligatory, should also provide a place for what is bad but not forbidden. For if there is such a thing as 'non-obligatory well-doing' then it is plausible to suppose that there is also such a thing as 'permissive ill-doing.' There is no term in moral literature, so far as I know, which has been used to designate just this latter class of

broadly: imperfect duties are said to be 'indeterminate' in that we have latitude with respect to the manner in which we fulfil them, whereas perfect duties are not thus 'indeterminate.' But if the distinction amounted only to this, then, surely, it would require us to say that *no* duties are perfect. If it is my duty to pay you ten dollars then I have latitude in that I may pay by cash, check, or money-order; or if it is my duty to pay you in cash, then I may pay by giving you a ten, or fives, or ones; or if it is my duty to give you a ten, then I may give you this one, that one, or the other one; or if it is my duty to give you this one, then I may hand it to you with the face looking up, or down, or right, or left; and so on *ad infinitum*.

actions; I shall refer to them as 'offences.'[7]

Just as it would be a mistake to identify supererogation with saintliness or heroism, so, too, it would be a mistake to identify what we may call the offensive with deviltry or villainy. And just as acts of supererogation, as well as duties, may be either trifling or heroic (or saintly), offences, as well as the forbidden, may be either trifling or villainous (or diabolical). If returning a handkerchief is both trifling and a duty then failure to return it is both trifling and forbidden; if a favour or an act of courtesy is trifling and supererogatory then a disfavour or an act of discourtesy is trifling and offensive.

We have a wealth of examples of what is both villainous (or diabolical) and forbidden. What would be a villainous offence — an act which is villainous, or heinous, and yet not forbidden? Many of the deeds of 'informers' seems to fall within this category. For example, suppose A knows concerning B, whom A dislikes, that the loss of B's employment would result in great tragedy for B and his family; that there is another man, C, who could do B's work but no more satisfactorily than B does it; and that B's employer, even if he knew the foregoing, would replace B by C if he thought that C were available. One might plausibly argue that, if A were deliberately to bring the availability of C to the attention of B's employer, his act would be permissible but at the same time heinous and inhuman.

The relation of the offensive to that which is forbidden is thus similar to that which has been said to hold between 'venial' and 'mortal' sins. A venial sin is, literally, a sin or misdeed which may be *pardoned*, or, as we might now say, *excused*.[8] St. Thomas wrote, for example:

> Venial sin is called a sin according to an imperfect notion of sin, and in

7. Other possible terms are 'faults,' 'misdemeanours,' 'moral torts,' 'peccadillos,' and 'venial sins' (to be discussed below), but these terms have, in their current uses, connotations which would make them misleading in the present context.

8. J. L. Austin contrasted justification and excuse by saying that, when we *justify* a questionable act 'we accept responsibility but deny that it was bad,' and that when we *excuse* an act 'we admit that it was bad but don't accept full, or even any, responsibility.' (*Philosophical Papers*, Oxford, 1961, p. 124). But if there are offences, 'venial misdeeds,' then we may also *excuse* an act, for which we do accept full responsibility, by admitting that it was bad but noting that it was only an offence — a misdeed which is permitted.

> relation to moral sin; even as an accident is called a being in relation to substance, according to an imperfect notion of being. For it is not *against* the law, since he who sins venially neither does what the law forbids, nor omits what the law prescribes to be done; but he acts *outside* the law, through not observing the mode of reason which the law intends.[9]

Offences, as we have said, are related to the forbidden in the way in which supererogation is related to the obligatory. But we must *not* suppose that an offence is to be equated with the failure to do what is supererogatory, or that the supererogatory is to be equated with the failure to do what would be an offence. This point becomes clear if we turn now to an alternative to the three-fold classification of moral concepts with which we began — even though, as I believe, the alternative is not entirely adequate.

5. The conceptual scheme to which I refer was suggested by Alexius Meinong, in his *Psychologisch-ethische Untersuchungen zur Werth-theorie* (Graz, 1894), and refined upon by Ernst Schwarz, in *Über den Wert, das Soll, und das richtige Werthalten* (Graz, 1934).

Meinong proposed that every act which is not morally indifferent may be put into one or another of the following four categories: the *meritorious*, the *required*, the *excusable*, and the *reprehensible* (or *inexcusable*).[10] The distinction between the meritorious and the required is very much like that between supererogation and the obligatory. Thus Meinong writes that 'there is considerable difference, within the sphere of the good, between the deeds of an Arnold von Winkelried or a Decius Mus and such activities as the ordinary performance of one's professional duties or the keeping of a promise.' (p. 89). The distinction between the excusable and the reprehensible, similarly, is very much like that between the offensive and the forbidden. (We might also say, though Meinong is not explicit on this point, that an indifferent act is one which falls outside of the four categories which Meinong mentions, a permitted act is one which is not reprehensible, and a non-obligatory act is one which is not

9. *Summa Theologica* I-II, Q. 88, Art. 1.

10. Meinong's terms were: *Das Verdienstliche, das Correcte, das Zulässige* and *das Verwerfliche*. I have chosen English terms which seem to me best to convey the sense of these terms as they were used by Meinong; I have used 'required' and not 'obligatory' in order not to prejudge the question whether Meinong's '*correct*' means the same as our 'obligatory.' Schwarz replaces '*verwerflich*' by '*unzulässig*' and uses '*korrekt*' in place of '*correct*.'

required.) Meinong proposes two theses relating his concepts, and Schwarz adds a third.

(1) Meinong suggests that the four concepts are related in a definite way with respect to what is good and what is bad: whatever is either meritorious or required is good; whatever is either excusable or reprehensible is bad; the meritorious is better than the required, the required is better than the excusable, and the excusable is better than the reprehensible.

(2) Schwarz now proposes that Meinong's four terms might be defined and formally related as follows: the meritorious is that which must be praised and may not be blamed; the required is that which may be praised and may not be blamed; the excusable is that which may not be praised and may be blamed; and the reprehensible is that which may not be praised and must be blamed. Schwarz then illustrates his proposal, along with Meinong's original suggestion, by means of the accompanying diagram (*op. cit.,* p. 60), which may be regarded as an alternative to the square of opposition with which we began. The area above the horizontal line is intended to represent what is good, that below is intended to represent what is bad; the diagonal expresses Meinong's ordering of the four types of act with respect to better and worse; and the midpoint represents those acts which are morally indifferent and which, presumably, may neither be praised nor be blamed.[11]

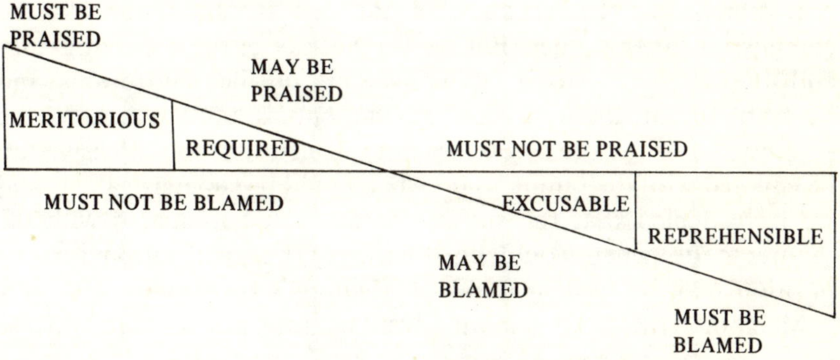

11. Compare Harald Ofstad, in 'The Function of Moral Philosophy,' in *Inquiry*, vol. I (1958) "a significant and fascinating area of moral philosophy is concerned with 'the advancement of *possible* conceptual systems for normative or evaluative ethics or for metaethics . . . Possible worlds are waiting to be explored" (pp. 48-9).

(3) Meinong proposes, finally, a suggestive 'law of omission' (*Unterlassungsgesetz*): for any act A, committing A is meritorious if and only if ommitting A is excusable, committing A is required if and only if omitting A is inexcusable (reprehensible), and omitting A is required if and only if committing A is inexcusable.[12]

It seems clear that Meinong intended his scheme to accommodate the kinds of moral fact which I have tried to outline. But if we equate his four categories — the meritorious, the required, the excusable and the reprehensible, respectively — with what we have been calling the supererogatory, the obligatory, the offensive and the forbidden, then, I think, we must reject each of the three theses just considered.

We cannot say that the supererogatory must be better than the obligatory, the obligatory better that the offensive, or the offensive better than the forbidden. For we have said that obligatory heroism may be better than trifling supererogation, and a villainous offence worse than what is trifling but forbidden.

We must reject Schwarz's proposal on similar grounds. We do not wish to say that trifling supererogation is more praiseworthy than the heroic performance of one's duty, or that what is trifling but forbidden is more blameworthy than a diabolic or villainous offence.

And, thirdly, we must reject Meinong's 'law of omission' in its application to two of our concepts. We *can* say of the obligatory and the forbidden (what Meinong says of the required and the reprehensible) that the omission of the one is tantamount to the commission of the other. But we can *not* say of the supererogatory and the offensive (what Meinong says of the meritorious and excusable) that the omission of the one is tantamount to the commission of the other. For we have denied that the offensive can be equated with the failure to do what would be supererogatory, and we have denied that the supererogatory can be equated with the failure to do what would be offensive. The justification for our position may be seen in terms of Meinong's own example.

Meinong writes: 'To gain an advantage for oneself at the expense

12. *Op. cit.*, pp. 89ff. Meinong's uncompleted *Ethische Bausteine*, in *Gesamtausgabe*, Band III, contains a more detailed discussion of this law. Compare: Francis Hutcheson's *Inquiry concerning the Original of our Ideas of Virtue of Moral Good* (1725), section VII; pp. 168-9 in vol. I of L.A. Selby-Bigge's *British Moralists*, Oxford 1897; also Richard Price, *A Review of the Principal Questions in Morals,* 3rd ed., 1787; 201-2 in D.D. Raphael's edition, Oxford 1943.

of another person may be excusable, within certain limits — for example, when the other person is one's competitor in business, but to step aside, in order that one's competitor may derive some benefit, would seem to be an act worthy of being called meritorious.'[13] It is plausible to suppose that the first of these acts is an offence; Meinong's successful business man may have been applying those stratagems of gamesmanship which enable one to 'win without actually cheating.'[14] And the business man who steps aside on behalf of his competitor certainly seems to be performing an act of supererogation. But Meinong is mistaken in supposing that the examples illustrate his 'law of omission.' Clearly at least four possibilities are involved and not, as Meinong appears to assume, only two. The four possibilities are: (i) doing something which will bring positive harm to a competitor; (ii) refraining from causing him any positive harm; (iii) doing something which will bring positive benefit to the competitor; and (iv) refraining from causing him any positive benefit. To equate the omission of an offence with the commission of the supererogatory, and the omission of the supererogatory with the commission of an offence, would be to assume, mistakenly, that (i) may be equated with (iv), and (ii) with (iii).

It may be asked, incidentally, whether the performance of a given act A entails the nonperformance of the nonperformance of A, and whether the nonperformance of A entails the performance of the nonperformance of A. If these entailments held, we could say of an offence of commission, for example, that it involves an offence of omission, viz., the offensive omission of the omission of the offensive commission, and analogously for the other moral categories. But it seems clear at least that nonperformance should not be said to entail performance of nonperformance; deliberately refraining from showing gratitude would exemplify performance of nonperformance. The latter could be an offence and the former not. Hence the example of the competitors above involves six possibilities rather than four, since each of the two cases we have called 'refraining' should be subdivided into 'deliberately refraining from doing' and 'not doing but not deliberately refraining from doing.'[15]

13. *Psychologisch-ethische Untersuchungen*, etc., p. 90.

14. This point was suggested to me by Wesley Salmon.

15. Meinong saw this latter point. The manuscript of his *Ethische Bausteine* contains the following remarks: 'One may ask whether the

Meinong's scheme recalls a useful clue: in considering how to classify any particular act, we must consider what would be the moral status, not only of its commission, but also of its omission: we should consider both performance and nonperformance.

I shall now propose an alternative conceptual scheme.

6. Let us make use of a pair of moral terms which may be construed as contraries — terms which are mutually exclusive but not contradictory. Among the available pairs are: *praiseworthy* and *blameworthy; meritorious* and *demeritorious;* Brantano's *worthy-of-love* and *worthy-of-hate; worthy-of-approval* and *worthy-of-disapproval; morally positive* and *morally negative; right* and *wrong;* and, simply, *good* and *bad*. Let us take the latter pair and interpret them as they would ordinarily be taken in such expressions as 'That would be a good thing to do' or 'That would be a bad thing to do,' where, it is essential to note, they are applied to *actions* and not to *agents* or to *consequences* of actions.

For every act that might be performed, then, there are at least three possibilities: (i) that it would be a good thing to do; (ii) that it would be a bad thing to do; and (iii) that it would be neither a good thing nor a bad thing to do. Thus we also make use of a three-fold classification. But let us note further that 'good' and 'bad' are applicable not only to commission, or performance; they are also applicable to omission, or nonperformance.

essential features of the law of omission are to be found in the law of double negation or in same analogues thereof. In such a case omission of omission would yield commission, just as the negation of a negation yields an affirmation; then, not only would the omission of the required be reprehensible, but the omission of the omission of the required would itself be required. But omission is not to be conceived in this way. For it is easy to see that the analogy between omission and negation breaks down just in the case of such reiteration. One may say of an omission, that when the opportunity or occasion to do something or to set out to do something arises, no use is made of the opportunity, either because there is no will to do it or because the subject deliberately refrains from doing what (he supposes) he could do if he chose. Perhaps the first of these two possibilities is more readily likened to negation than is the second. But it is not possible, in this first case, to conceive what an omission of the omission would be' (pp. 33-34). Compare also L. Nelson, *System of Ethics*, section 24, New Haven, 1956 (transl. from the German, Leipzig, 1917).

If now we are to arrive at an adequate classification of moral concepts, I suggest we must so interpret 'good' and 'bad' in their present use that their application to performance is logically independent of their application to non-performance; that is to say, 'It would be good to do A' does not imply 'It would be bad not to do A,' and 'It would be bad to do A' does not imply 'It would be good not to do A.'

Let us now say that an act is *obligatory*, or a *duty*, if it would be good to do and bad not to do. And let us say that an act is *forbidden*, in the sense in wich we have been taking this term, if it would be bad to do and good not to do.[16] Hence performance is obligatory if and only if nonperformance is forbidden, and performance is forbidden if and only if nonperformance is obligatory.

An act, the performance of which is *supererogatory*, may now be described as something which it would be good to do and neither good nor bad not to do. An act, the *non*performance of which is supererogatory, would thus be something which it is good not to do and neither good nor bad to do. (Our examples of supererogation, up to now, have been examples of supererogatory performance. People not demanding their rights provide us with obvious cases of supererogatory nonperformance).

An offensive performance, or *offence of commission*, now becomes something which it would be bad to do and neither good nor bad not to do; and an offensive nonperformance, or *offence of omission*, something which it would be bad not to do and neither good nor bad to do.

An example may help us now to contrast supererogatory commission and omission with offences of commission and omission. If the waiter is not busy, failure to tell him that he has brought the wrong desert may be supererogatory omission; but if he is told and then returns with the proper desert, failure to say 'Thank you' may be an offence of omission; a generous tip would then be supererogatory commission and a complaint to the manager an offence of commission.

An *indifferent* act — one which is 'totally indifferent' — would now become on such that performance is neither good nor bad and

16. We may leave undecided the question whether it is better to *define* the terms 'obligatory' and 'forbidden' in this way or to define them in the way suggested in section 2 above.

nonperformance neither good nor bad. Hence we have a way of distinguishing the supererogatory — and the offensive — from the indifferent.

We may continue to say, as before, that an act is *permitted* provided only it is not forbidden, and that an act is *unrequired*, or nonobligatory, provided only that it is not obligatory. Thus offensive commission and offensive omission are permitted, just as supererogatory commission and supererogatory omission are unrequired.

There remain two possibilities: those acts such that both their omission and commission would be good, and those such that both their omission and commission would be bad. Each of these suggests a kind of moral perplexity, the first but not the second a state of blessedness. There are no terms, so far as I know, that have been used to designate just these two categories. Let us say that acts of the first type — those things which it would be good to do and also good not to do — are *totally supererogatory*; and let us say, similarly, that acts of the second type — those things which it would be bad to do and also bad not to do — are *totally offensive* (thus using 'totally' in a way analogous to that in which it is used in the theory of relations). What would exemplify these categories? There are at least two possibilities.

(i) A strict utilitarianism, or ethics of consequence, would require us to say that, if there were an act such that its performance would increase the amount of value in the world and such that its nonperformance would increase the amount of value in the world by exactly the same amount, then that act would be 'totally supererogatory,' as defined. If the only morally relevant consequences of a contemplated act would be that its performance would bring about a certain amount of pleasure to one person and its nonperformance would bring about that same amount of pleasure to another person then, on a strictly utilitarian ethics, the act would be totally supererogatory. Replacing 'pleasure' by 'displeasure,' we could similarly describe an act which would be totally offensive.

(ii) If promise-keeping is always good, and if it is possible to promise a tautological act (e.g. 'I promise either to go or not to go'), then it is possible to find an act (in this instance, my going) which is totally supererogatory. And if promise-breaking is always bad, and if it is possible to promise a contradiction (e.g. 'I promise to go now and not to go now'), then it is possible to find an act (again, my going) which would be totally offensive. Other non-utilitarian rules provide similar possibilities.

Our classification may now be put more schematically. I have said that to determine the moral status of any particular act we must decide (*a*) whether its performance would be good, bad, or neither good nor bad, and (*b*) whether its nonperformance would be good, bad, or neither good nor bad. For any act, therefore, there are nine possibilities, which are represented in the accompanying table. The letters 'g,' 'b,' and 'n,' respectively, stand for 'good,' 'bad,' and 'neither good nor bad' (= 'neutral'); they are paired in such a way that the first member of each pair refers to performance, the second to nonperformance.

1. b, b Totally offensive
2. b, n Offence of commission
3. b, g Forbidden
4. n, b Offence of omission
5. n, n Totally indifferent
6. n, g Supererogatory omission
7. g, b Obligatory
8. g, n Supererogatory commission
9. g, g Totally supererogatory.

It would be possible, of course, to replace the table by still another diagram.

We may now suggest, very briefly, the way in which this table might be used to classify moral systems.

7. The richest moral system would be one allowing all nine possibilities to be exemplified. The poorest system would be one allowing none to be exemplified; such a system would imply that there are no acts, and perhaps should not be called a moral system at all. (Determinism might be said to imply a system of the latter sort.) According to certain nihilistic moralities, only the fifth possibility — total indifference — is capable of being exemplified. According to utilitarianism, in the strict sense of this term, the even-numbered lines are to be excluded, since strict utilitarianism implies that, for any act, if its performance is better than its nonperformance, its performance is obligatory, and if its nonperformance is better than its performance, its performance is forbidden.[17] But the strict utilitarian may

17. 'Certainly we should agree that a truly moral man cannot say to himself "This is the best thing on the whole for me to do, but yet it is not my duty to do it though it is within my power"; this would certainly seem to common sense an immoral paradox.' Sidgwick *The Methods of Ethics*, 6th ed., London, 1901, p. 220.

be able to find instances of each of the odd-numbered possibilities. A moral system more rigorous than strict utilitarianism would allow for the possibility of only lines three and seven, thus classifying every act as being either obligatory or forbidden.[18] For some of us, it seems plausible to suppose that all of these categories, with the possible exceptions of the first and the last, are capable of being exemplified. This view, since it implies that there may be both permissive ill-doing and nonobligatory well-doing, is certainly latitudinarian. We may think of such a morality as being laid down by a charitable Lawgiver who, in an act of supererogatory omission, refrains from commanding what is too difficult.[19] A Lawgiver who was even more charitable, or more lenient, might provide only for supererogation, offences and the totally indifferent; still another Lawgiver might provide only for supererogation and the indifferent; still another for supererogation alone. More rigid Lawgivers would restrict themselves to the first five possibilities or to some subclass thereof.

Since there are nine possibilities for every act, we could continue until we had described 512 possible moral systems, but most of these would be of little interest. And by replacing our pair of contraries, 'good' and 'bad,' with other pairs, e.g. 'meritorious' and 'demeritorious,' we could classify acts in still other ways and multiply the number of possible systems *ad infinitum.* But I think that 'good' and 'bad,' if they are taken in the way I have suggested above, provide us with the system we set out to find.

8. Let us now reduce our ethical terms to one — to 'ought to be' — and summarize the relations which hold among them.

Some possible situations or states of affairs are such that it *ought to*

18. In his discussion 'Of the Bad Principle in Human Nature,' in the first part of *Die Religion innerhalb der Grenzen der bloßen Vernunft*, Kant says that it is in general 'important for Ethics to admit, as far as possible, no intermediates, either in actions or in human characters . . . Those who are attached to this strict view are commomly called *rigourists* (a name that is meant as reproach, but which is really praise): and their antipodes, who may be called *latitudinarians*.' *Kant's Critique of Practical Reason and Other Works*, ed. by T.K. Abbott, 6th ed., London, 1959, p. 329.

19. Acts of trifling supererogation are not difficult to perform; but it would be difficult for anyone to perform *all* of those acts of trifling supererogation that are in his power; similarly for the omission of trifling offences.

be that they exist, and others are such that it ought to be that they do not exist. A particular act which might be performed on a specific occasion is something which it is *good* to perform provided that the situation which the act would bring about is one which ought to exist; the act is something which it is *bad* to perform provided that the situation is one which ought not to exist. The *obligatory* is that which it is good to do and bad not to do; the *forbidden* is that which it is obligatory not to do; and the *permitted* is that which it is not forbidden to do. We may say, if we like, that those acts which are neither obligatory nor forbidden are *optional*. The *indifferent*, however, is that which it is neither good nor bad to do and neither good nor bad not to do. The *supererogatory* is that which is good but not obligatory to do and the *offensive* that which is bad but not forbidden.[20]

20. I am indebted for suggestions and corrections to John T. Stevenson, John Ladd, Richard Schmitt and John W. Lenz; it was Mr. Stevenson who first presented me with the problem of this paper.

BEGINNINGS AND ENDINGS

Introduction

The philosophy of Brentano is scientific and empirical, and it is also analytic in the best sence of this term — that is to say, in the sense in which the *Metaphysics* of Aristotle may be said to be analytic. For analytic philosophy is opposed, not to metaphysics, but to undisciplined and irresponsible ways of thinking about philosophy. In the present paper, I will illustrate the way in which Brentano applied the techniques of philosophical analysis to one of the most perplexing areas of metaphysics — a set of *aporiae* about motion and rest and about coming into being and passing away. These questions which were suggested by Aristotle were discussed at length by philosophers in the scholastic tradition. And they led Mendelssohn — at least, according to the way in which Kant interprets him — to conclude that the soul is immortal. The best answers, it seems to me, are those that were suggested by Brentano.

The Plerosis of Temporal Boundaries

I will set forth Brentano's theory about the "plerosis" of temporal boundaries. Then I will try to show how this theory may be used to deal with the *aporiae* in question including that which led to Mendelssohn's attempted proof. What Brentano did here was to make certain suggestions and to point the way. In what follows, I will carry out these suggestions and supply details that are left implicit by Brentano. The best statement of Brentano's own views on these topics may be found in his *Philosophische Untersuchungen zu Raum, Zeit und Kontinuum.*[1]

The *plerosis* — or *fullness* — of a boundary is a function of the number of directions in which it is a boundary. Thus a boundary within a temporal continuum may be a boundary in one direction (if

1. Franz Brentano, *Philosophische Untersuchungen zu Raum, Zeit und Kontinuum*, Hamburg: Felix Meiner 1976, ed., Stephan Körner and Roderick M. Chisholm.

it is merely the endpoint of something that is past or if it is merely the beginning point of something that is future). Or it may be a boundary in two directions (if it is both an endpoint and a beginning point). But the boundary of a spatial continuum is not thus restricted with respect to the number of directions in which it may be a boundary. It may be a boundary in all the directions in which it is capable of being a boundary, or it may be a boundary in only some of these directions. If a boundary — whether temporal or spatial — is a boundary in all the directions in which it is capable of being a boundary, then it exists in "full plerosis"; otherwise it exists only in "partial plerosis." Brentano believes that by means of the concept of plerosis he can speak in a certain sense of the "parts" of a boundary even though the boundary may have no dimensions.[2] It is one thing to speak of the present as being the end of the past and another thing to speak of the present as being the beginning of the future.

Let us now consider the first of our problems.[3]

"If a thing begins to move is there a last moment of its being at rest or a first moment of its being in motion? There cannot be both, for if there were, then there would be a time between the two moments, and at *that* time the thing could be said neither to be at rest nor to be in motion."

The statement of the problem, Brentano would say, correctly recognizes the *impossibility of adjacent points* But what it fails to recognize is *the possibility of coincident points*.[4] Brentano's solution is to say that at one and the same moment the thing ceases to be at rest and begins to be in motion. The temporal boundary of the thing's being at rest (the end of its being at rest) is the same as the temporal boundary of the thing's being in motion (the beginning of its being in motion), but the boundary is twofold (*zweiteilig*) with respect to its plerosis. The boundary is in half plerosis (*in halber Plerose*) at rest and in half plerosis in motion.

2. On the relation between the *boundaries* of things and the *parts* of things, see Brentano's *Kategorienlehre,* Hamburg: Felix Meiner 1968, 171n.; *The Theory of Categories,* The Hague: Martinus Nijhoff 1981, 128n.

3. Concerning these problems compare: Norman Kretzmann, "Socrates is Whiter than Plato begins to be White," *Nous*, XI (1977), 3-15; "Incipit/Desinit," in *Motion and Time, Space and Matter*, ed. P.K. Machamer and R.G. Turnbull, Columbus: Ohio State University Press 1976, 101-36.

4. See *Psychology from an Empirical Standpoint*, p. 357.

One may object: How can the introduction of a new technical term solve the problem? I would suggest that the introduction of a new technical term *can* be used to solve a problem, provided that the technical term can be used to explicate some of the terms in which the problem is originally formulated. I believe this is the case with Brentano's term "plerosis."

To see that this is so, let us replace Brentano's plerosis-vocabulary by a slightly different terminology.

Reformulation of the Doctrine of Temporal Plerosis

We shall assume with Brentano that *motion within a period of time* is conceptually prior to *motion within an instant* and hence that the latter concept is to be explicated in terms of the former. We shall also assume with Brentano that the nature of a boundary is entirely dependent upon that which it bounds.[5]

Consider a thing that is in motion and consider any point or instant of time that falls within the period that the thing is in motion. If an instant thus falls within a time that a thing A is moving, then: either (a) the instant bounds a prior but not a subsequent motion of A, or (b) the instant bounds a subsequent but not a prior motion of A, or (c) the instant bounds both a prior and a subsequent motion of A.

Given the general principle according to which the nature of a boundary is determined by the nature of that which it bounds, we may characterize motion at an instant by reference to motion within the periods of time that are bounded by the instant. Motion within a period of time, then, will be an undefined concept; but the above concepts, all involving motion at an instant, may be defined in terms of motion within a period of time.

Thus we may say:

> t bounds a prior motion of A =Df There is a time prior to t which is such that A moves during every period of time between it and t

Thus if t is the present moment and bounds a prior motion of A, then there has been a period of time such that A was moving during that period of time and also at every period of time that there has been since that time.

5. For a discussion of these questions which is not based upon either of these assumptions, see Philip L. Quinn, "Persistence throughout an Interval of Time and Existence at an Instant of Time," *Ratio*, XXI (1979), 1-12.

t bounds a subsequent motion of A =Df There is a time subsequent to t which is such that A moves during every period of time between it and t

If t is the present moment and bounds a subsequent motion of A, then there will be a period of time such that A will be moving during that period of time and also at every period of time that there will be before that time.

Aristotle says, in the *Physics*, that "there cannot be any irreducible period of time which in its entirety is the 'first' period of the change, since there is no limit to the divisions of a period, and so you can always show that the change was already taking place before the whole of any period, however minute, has passed."[6] And he concludes, similarly, that "being brought to rest is an experience that occupies time."[7]

But given the above analysis, we may say what it is for a point of time — a temporal boundary — to be the point at which motion begins, and we may say what it is for a point of time to be the point at which motion ends.

A begins to move at t =Df t bounds a subsequent but not a prior motion of A

A ceases to move at t =Df t bounds a prior but not a subsequent motion of A.

Our definitions enable us to say that the time at which a thing *begins to move* is the same as the time at which it *ceases to rest*, and that the time at which a thing *begins to rest* is the same as that at which it *ceases to move*. And these statements are not contradictory.

One may ask: "If the thing both begins to move and also ceases to rest at t, then is it in motion at t or is it at rest at t? And if it begins to rest at t and also ceases to move at t, then is it in motion at t or is it at rest at t?" We find the answer to these questions if we say what it is for a thing to move at an instant t:

A is in motion at an instant t =Df Either t bounds a subsequent motion of A, or t bounds a prior motion of A.

The answer to our questions now becomes: "At the instant at which the thing begins to move and also ceases to rest, the thing is in motion. And at the instant at which it ceases to move and begins to rest, it is also in motion.

6. *Physics*, Book VI, Chapter 5, 236a.
7. *Physics*, Book VI, Chapter 8, 238b.

Application to a Further Problem

The second of our problems may be put as follows. "Suppose a body is thrown straight up in the air and is prevented from deviating from its path. Is it at rest for a moment between the time it stops going up and starts to go down (and if so how long?) or does it start to go down at the same moment it stops going up?"

Possibly the orthodox way of dealing with this problem would be to say something like this: There is no last instant at which the object was going up and no first instant at which it was going down. But there was one instant which was later than all the instants at which it was in motion upwards and earlier than all the instances in which it was in motion downwards. And we may interpret this view in such a way that it is consistent with Brentano's theory.[8] But let us try to spell out Brentano's theory in detail, for it is a part of a more general ontology which, I believe, is of first importance.

Brentano writes: "We should not assume that there is here a moment of complete rest. There is, rather, a moment wherein the beginning of the object's fall coincides with the cessation of its going up."[9] He says that at that moment the motion of the thing is "in half plerosis" with respect to going up and "in half plerosis" with respect to going down.

If our suggestion above is correct, we could rephrase Brentano's solution this way. When we say, of any moment, that the thing is going up at that moment, then we leave open three possibilities for that moment: either (a) it bounds both a prior and a subsequent upward movement; or (b) it bounds a prior but not a subsequent upward movement; or (c) it bounds a subsequent but not a prior upward movement. And analogously for going down.

Thus we may distinguish six different situations that obtain during the motion of the thing in question. (i) There is a moment which bounds a subsequent motion of the thing but not a prior motion of

8. Peter van Inwagen notes that the most natural way to describe the motion of a see-saw would be similar. "There was no last instant at which the see-saw tilted to the left and no last instant at which it tilted to the right. But there was one instant which was later than all the instants at which it tilted to the left and earlier than all the instants at which it tilted to the right." Brentano's concepts, of course, are readily applicable to this situation.

9. The quotation is from a brief undated manuscript of Brentano's entitled "Plerose" and classified in Brentano's *Nachlaß* as Megethologie 15.

the thing; this is the moment at which the thing begins to move. (ii) There are moments which bound both prior and subsequent upward motions; these will occur after the moment at which the thing begins to move and before it reaches its highest point. (iii) There is a moment which bounds a prior but not a subsequent *upward* motion; this will be the moment at which the thing reaches the highest point. (iv) There is a moment which bounds a subsequent but not a prior *downward* motion; this will be the moment at which the thing leaves the highest point. (v) There are moments which bound both prior and subsequent downward motions; these will occur after the moment the thing leaves the highest point and before it stops moving. And (vi) there is a moment which bounds a prior but not a subsequent downward motion; this is the moment at which it ceases to move.[10]

Brentano's suggestion may now be construed as telling us that the moment of (iii) and the moment of (iv) are one and the same. The moment at which the thing changes its course is one that bounds a prior upward motion and also a bounds a subsequent downward motion.

Brentano says that, if the body rises and falls in a straight line (and in a path that is not elliptical), then the path has a highest point. Temporally, this highest point is "a kind of null-point of rising and falling. But it is not to be called a point of rest, for there is motion up to and beyond that point (it is a point which bounds two motions — an upward motion and a downward motion)."[11]

"Are you saying, then, that when the thing is at the apex it is going up and going down at one and the same time?" The answer requires that we make a distinction. If, in saying that something is "going up at a certain moment" we mean that the moment bounds a prior upward motion and *also* a subsequent upward motion, then we should *not* say that the thing is going up at that moment; and analogously for "going down." But if, in saying that a thing is "going up at a certain

10. Or if we leave open the possibility that the thing bounces and immediately goes up again, we will say: "There is a moment which bounds a prior but not a subsequent downward motion, and this is the moment at which the thing ceases to go down."

11. The quotation is taken from Brentano's lecture notes on "Psychognosie," which he used in Vienna during the academic year 1890-1891. These notes are catalogued in Brentano's *Nachlaß* as E L 74; the quotation is taken from section 33.

moment," we mean that the moment bounds *either* a prior upward motion *or* a subsequent upward motion, then we *may* say that the thing is going up at that moment; and analogously for "going down." Hence if we take "going up" and "going down" in the first sense, then we should say that, when the thing is at the apex, it is neither going up nor going down. But if we take them in the second sense then we may, without contradiction, say that the thing is both going up and going down.

Mendelssohn's Attempted Proof

Brentano's solution applies in an obvious way to our third problem, which is the source of Mendelssohn's attempted proof of the immortality of the soul.

Kant expounds Mendelssohn's argument this way:

> His argument is that since the soul cannot be diminished, and so gradually lose something of its existence, being by degrees changed into nothing (for since it has no parts, it has no multiplicity in itself), there would be no time between a moment in which it is and another in which it is not — which is impossible.[12]

Kant thought that the way to refute Mendelssohn was to suppose that there are degrees of reality. Then we could say that a substance

> may be changed into nothing, not indeed by dissolution, but by gradual loss (*remissio*) of its powers, and so, if I may be permitted the use of the term, by elanguescence.[13]

Brentano saw that Mendelssohn's argument was inconclusive and that Kant's doctrine, with its suggestion that there might be a mean between being and nonbeing, is absurd.[14] Mendelssohn's argument can be dealt with in a much more satisfactory way by means of Brentano's analysis of the nature of boundaries.

Let us summarize the problem as follows:

"If a thing ceases to be, then either there is a last moment of its existence or there is a first moment of its nonexistence, but there cannot be both. Which, then, is there?"[15]

12. *Critique of Pure Reason*, B413-414; N. Kemp Smith edition, 372-3.
13. *Op. cit.*, B414; Kemp Smith, 373.
14. See Brentano's *Kategorienlehre*, 90-97; *Theory of Categories*, 73-7.
15. This problem is discussed in detail by F. Suarez, *Metaphysicae*

Brentano is able to say that there is *both* a last moment of existence and a first moment of nonexistence; they are one and the same. This may be seen by modifying the definitions we have given above concerning the beginning and ending of motion. Those definitions pertain to motion and rest, but they may be adapted to existence and nonexistence. We make assumptions that are analogous to those that we made in the case of motion: *existence during a period of time* is conceptually prior to *existence at an instant*; and the nature of a boundary is dependent upon the nature of that which it bounds.

We presuppose, then, the concept of existing during a period of time. And in terms of this concept we characterize what may be said about existence — and nonexistence — at an instant.

The definitions that follow presuppose the concept of a thing existing throughout a period of time — a stretch of time that is not an instant.

> t bounds a prior period of A's existence =Df There is a time prior to t which is such that A exists during all periods of time between it and t

> t bounds a subsequent period of A's existence =Df There is a period of time subsequent to t which is such A exists during all periods of time between it and t

Now we may speak of the time at which A begins to exist and of the time at which A ceases to exist:

> A begins to exist at t =Df t bounds a subsequent but not a prior period of A's existence.

> A ceases to exist at t =Df t bounds a prior but not a subsequent period of A's existence.

Our definitions allow us to say that "the first moment of a thing's existence" is the same as "the last moment of the thing's first period of nonexistence," and that "the last moment of a thing's existence" is the same as "the first moment of the thing's second period of nonexistence."

One may ask: "If an instant t is the first moment of a thing's existence and the last moment of its nonexistence, then should we say

Disputationes, Disp. 50, Section 2, Paragraphs 10-16. Compare Thomas Aquinas, *Summa Theologica*, Part III, Q.75, Art. 7; Part I-II, Q. 113, Art. 7; Part. I, Q. 53, Art. 3.

that the thing exists at t or that it does not exist at t? Or if t is the last moment of a thing's existence and the first moment of its non-existence, then should we say that the thing exists at t or that it does not exist at t?"

The question is, actually: "What does it mean to say of a thing that it *exists at an instant*?" Hence the question is like one we might have asked about motion: "I know what it is for a thing to move throughout an extended period of time. But what is it for a thing to *move at an instant*?" Just as we had characterized motion at an instant by reference to motion through a period of time, so, too, we can characterize existing at an instant by reference to existing through a period of time.

Let us say, then, what it is for a thing to exist at an instant t:

> A exists at an instant t =Df Either t bounds a subsequent period of A's existence, or t bounds a prior period of A's existence.

And so if t is the first moment of the thing's existence and the last moment of its nonexistence, then the thing exists at t. And if t is the last moment of the thing's existence and the first moment of its nonexistence, then the thing also exists at t.

Let us now consider the following objection to the thesis that there cannot be both a last moment of one's existence *and also* a first moment of one's (second period of) non-existence:

> If, then, we divide all instants of time, whether past, present, or future, into two series — those instants at which Socrates was alive, and those instants at which he was not alive — and leave out of consideration, for the sake of greater simplicity, all those instants before he lived, we see at once, by the simple application of Dedekind's Axiom, that if Socrates entered into eternal life after his death, there must have been either a last moment of his earthly life *or* a first moment of his eternal life, but not both.[16]

The reply is that "a moment at which Socrates was alive" only *appears* to be incompatible with "a moment at which Socrates was not alive." For the moments at which he was alive are of three different kinds: (i) moments such that he existed up to those moments and also from those moments on; (ii) a moment such that he existed from that moment on, but didn't exist from any moment up to that

16. Philip E.B. Jourdain, *The Philosophy of Mr. B*rtr*nd R*ss*ll*, London: George Allen & Unwin 1918, p. 49.

moment; and (iii) a moment such that he existed from a time up to that moment but didn't exist from that moment on. And the moments at which he was not alive (the moments of his second period of nonexistence) are of two different kinds: (iv) moments such that Socrates failed to exist at any time up to that moment and also failed to exist from that moment on; and (v) a moment such that Socrates did exist from a certain time up to that moment but did not exist from that moment on. The moments "at which Socrates was alive" will include (i), (ii), (iii), and (v); the moments "at which Socrates was not alive" will include (iv) and (v). Hence the two phrases are not contraries.

Therefore Brentano can say of Mendelssohn's proof:

> Kant misses the true weakness of this proof. According to Mendelssohn, it is contradictory to suppose that a simple substance ceases to be, since after the last moment of its existence there can be no first moment of its nonexistence. Mendelssohn does not note that one could prove the impossibility of breaking up a composite substance in a similar way: after that last moment at which its parts are together there can be no first moment at which they are separated. . . Actually, however, there is no contradiction. A temporal point as boundary of a one-dimensional continuum is twofold [*zweiteilig*] in respect of its plerosis. It is logically possible for something to exist up to and at a given period of time and from that same point on *not* to exist. It ceases to be and begins not to be in the same moment. There is no contradiction in supposing a simple substance to be annihilated (though this is ruled out by the general cosmological law according to which God never lets anything go to waste).[17]

In the lectures on metaphysics that Brentano gave at Würzburg between the years 1867 and 1870, he raised such questions as these:

"Consider that which is in the process of coming into being. Should we say that it exists at the time it is coming into being or that it does not exist at the time it is coming into being?"

"Consider that which ceases to be. Should we say that it exists when it ceases to be or that it does not exist when it ceases to be?"

In each case, the alternatives that are available seem to be unacceptable. At the time that he gave these lectures, Brentano was inclined to say that, strictly speaking, there *is* no coming into being

17. *Kategorienlehre* 93; *Theory of Categories*, 75.

and passing away.[18] But in saying this, he did not mean that everything exists eternally. He meant, rather, that although a thing may exist at certain times and not at others, there is no event which is that thing's coming into being, and no event which is that thing's passing away. But given his later concept of plerosis, he could say that the instant at which a thing comes into being is an instant at which it exists and that the instant at which it passes away is also one at which it exists.

18. The discussion appears on pages 50-52 of Brentano's "Würzburger Metaphysik Kolleg," classified as M96 among the unpublished manuscripts of Brentano.